CROSSCURRENTS *Modern Critiques*

Harry T. Moore, *General Editor*

Norman Friedman

e.e.cummings

The Growth of a Writer

With a Preface by Harry T. Moore

SOUTHERN ILLINOIS UNIVERSITY PRESS

Carbondale and Edwardsville

FEFFER & SIMONS, INC.

London and Amsterdam

IN MEMORIAM

Edward Estlin Cummings

1894–1962

Copyright © 1964 by Southern Illinois University Press

First published, March 1964
Second printing, September 1966
Third printing, December 1969
Arcturus Books edition, September 1980
All rights reserved
Printed in the United States of America
Designed by Andor Braun

Library of Congress Cataloging in Publication Data

Friedman, Norman.
    E. E. Cummings, the growth of a writer.

    (Arcturus books; 152)
    Bibliography: p.
    Includes index.
    1. Cummings, Edward Estlin, 1894–1962—Criticism and in-
terpretation.   I. Title.
[PS3505.U334Z66 1980]   811'.52   80-17081
ISBN 0-8093-0978-5 (pbk.)

PREFACE

FIRST: *if I don't use capitals for e. e. cummings, it isn't just a stunt. He had his name put legally into lower case, and in his later books the titles and his name were always in lower case. And I have a weakness for Edmund Wilson's rendition of cummings, in his Finnegans Wake parody, as hee hee cunnings. So be it—all this goes with the iconoclasm of the twenties, with its unpunctuated, uncapitalized poetry. The lower case is a kind of continuing talisman of cummings, though it doesn't embed him in the twenties. He comes through to us as what Norman Friedman, in the present book, calls him: "a serious poet." Mr. Friedman believes that cummings shouldn't be favored or disfavored because of his punctuative and typographical tricks, and he is quite right. In the foregoing I am merely entering the cummings atmosphere. That is merely incidental, however, to the fact that I do favor him.*

What else could be one's reaction to the creator of a lyric as nearly perfect as the one beginning, "since feeling is first"?—and there are a few hundred others. One critical canard says that cummings didn't grow as a poet; happily, Mr. Friedman's book, whose subtitle is The Growth of a Writer, is a study of the vision and development of cummings. It takes up the challenge in its very first paragraph and then carefully proceeds to show how cummings did grow.

We wanted a book on cummings in this series. I had read Mr. Friedman on the subject and knew that he was just the critic to provide such a volume for us; it is in itself a development beyond his earlier work on cummings, and a volume we are in every way delighted to have in the series.

As Mr. Friedman unhappily notes, e. e. cummings died as the manuscript of this book was being typed; Mr. Friedman had had the benefit of many discussions with the poet, but not, regrettably, of his comments on the manuscript of the present volume.

Although cummings died at sixty-eight, he hardly seemed aged to those who saw him in his later years. As Charles Norman notes in his cummings biography, The Magic Maker (Macmillan, 1958), cummings in New York went out even in the severest winter days, leaving his Patchin Place home to walk to Washington Square, where he sat sketching.

Many of us were priviledged to hear cummings deliver i: six nonlectures at Sanders Memorial Theater, Harvard University, in 1952–53. It is safe to use the word many, because the hall was crowded for each of cummings' appearances, and finally there was standing room only. Harvard students and teachers and numerous citizens of Cambridge and Boston found that a cummings lecture (rather, nonlecture) was an exciting experience. I don't know how many of them felt, as I did, that it was a more exciting experience than even T. S. Eliot or Dylan Thomas could provide.

A tall man, balding, read the lectures; his voice was low, in its pronunciation an example of the "accent" known as Ha'v'd. I had once written (for Poetry magazine) about cummings' recordings of his own work and had spoken of his voice as having raised eyebrows. It had, really. And cummings was one of the great readers of poetry. Like Eliot, he was on the quiet side, but without Eliot's suggestion of elegant weariness. Of course cummings didn't have the plangency and flamboyance of Dylan Thomas, but I find his readings just as satisfactory. Anyhow who hasn't heard them has missed a treat.

Records of the nonlectures apparently haven't been

published, which is unfortunate; they were taped and broadcast at the time, and they should be issued in order to present cummings viva voce, as anyone will agree who has heard his poetry records or who attended those Cambridge presentations. Fortunately the nonlectures have been printed, first by Harvard University Press in 1953 and then by Atheneum in a paperback in 1962. They make excellent reading, for—at the suggestion of Norman Friedman—they were largely autobiographical, "the exploration of my stance as a writer." As Mr. Friedman shows in the present book, the poet examined various phases of his experience, and then at the end of each session he read some poems by others. And here is where he was particularly brilliant vocally, for he gave us not only Keats and Wordsworth and Shakespeare and Donne as we had never quite heard them before, but also various poems of other tongues. He read German and Italian (Dante) with musical ease, and confidently dropped into medieval French and English verse. This was more than just a virtuoso performance: cummings read the poems out of deep love. And one could only reflect how much a part of the long poetic tradition cummings really was. An innovator, certainly, both in his technique and the freshness of his vision—of which Mr. Friedman will have much to say later—but above all he was an important lyricist. Did I quote Mr. Friedman as saying that cummings was "a serious poet"? Please note that he also calls him a great one.

Before leaving the subject of cummings in Mr. Friedman's extremely capable hands, I want to quote just one of cummings' poems, one of my favorites because it is so instinctively cummingsian. It is a verse written sometime in his childhood and preserved by his mother, who gave it to Charles Norman for his biography:

> O, the pretty birdie,O
> with his little toe,toe,toe!

There is much of the later poet in that couplet, which is a testimony to his lifelong vision and a proof that the mode in which he wrote was natural to him, not an assumed or eccentric manner. How marvelously that bird makes his three little hops. This is kinetic, as cummings' writing always was, with the music and visualization wonderfully matched. It is moving to see how the gift operated so naturally in the child who was to become a poet.

Earlier, I spoke of cummings as not seeming aged. He seemed joyously youthful, despite the baldness, when delivering the nonlectures. In the present book, Mr. Friedman points out that cummings' 95 Poems (Harcourt, Brace, 1958) seemed remarkably vigorous for a man of sixty-four. Now, just as I am about to return to the compositor the proofsheets of the present volume, a last book of cummings' verse has come in, soon to be published by Harcourt, Brace and World: 73 poems, I hope they aren't the last seventy-three, for they show how brilliantly cummings wrote in his later years. A few of the poems seem a little tricksy, but there are some lyrics which will stand among cummings' best. The eight-line satire beginning "annie died the other day" is cummings at his most mischievous; and the seventy-third and final, poem (beginning "all worlds have halfsight,seeing either with") makes a joyous epitaph for e. e. cummings, himself a "citizen of ecstasies" who in these fourteen lines looks on life and on death and does so with joy.

All the rest of cummings' poems—in the Collected edition and 95 Poems—are discussed with expertness, and with critical joy, by Mr. Friedman, who treats all cummings' books in this full and notable study. It deals not only with the poet's lyric and comic aspects, but very importantly examines the "basic mystical insight which is the real foundation of his work." Twentieth-century readers owe e. e. cummings a great debt for being the grand and joyful poet that he was; they also owe a debt to Mr. Friedman for interpreting all his writings so valuably.

HARRY T. MOORE

Southern Illinois University
October 26, 1963

ACKNOWLEDGMENTS

IT IS my unhappy duty to record the fact that E. E. Cummings died just as the manuscript of this book was being typed. Therefore, although I wrote to and talked with him about it, I did not enjoy the privilege of receiving his reactions to and comments on the text itself. That the world has lost a great poet, one who was growing right up to the very last, it is the intention of this book to underscore. I have let the manuscript stand mainly as it was written.

Since, however, I have already published *E. E. Cummings: The Art of His Poetry* (The Johns Hopkins Press, 1960), perhaps a word of explanation is due. That book was conceived primarily as a formal study of the poetry, and hence its main topics are technical. The poet's vision and development are considered, but are subordinated to these topics. In the present book, though, vision and development are the primary concerns, and hence technical matters are treated mainly as they illuminate these concerns. (Not that vision and technique are separable; in each case, I have treated them in relationship to one another, merely shifting the emphasis as the focus of attention shifts.) Since this is so, the present book tries to cover all of Cummings' writings, and not just the poetry.

Moreover, each book, in having a different purpose and a different organization, is intended for a somewhat different audience. The first one is designed basically for my fellow critics and teachers, while the present book, although not a popularization, is planned more as an introductory survey and aims at a somewhat broader audience. This book, in sum, is not merely a re-working of the other. There is, indeed, very little overlap between them, for they are two separate books and all of Cummings' work, including the poetry, was re-studied for this purpose.

For permission to use portions of four of Cummings' un-published letters, many thanks are due to Mr. Alexander P. Clark, Curator of Manuscripts, Princeton University Library, where the letters are on deposit; Mr. Allen Tate, to whom three of them are addressed; Mr. Jonathan Bishop, to whose father, the late John Peale Bishop, one of them is addressed; and Marion Morehouse Cummings, the poet's widow. I am also grateful to the University of Connecticut Research Foundation for the award of a small grant to make the trip to Princeton.

For permission to use published material, gratitude is expressed to the following: Mrs. Cummings and Harcourt, Brace and World, Mr. Charles Norman (from *The Magic Maker: E. E. Cummings*, © Charles Norman 1958), and Harvard University Press (from *i:six nonlectures*, copyright 1953 by E. E. Cummings).

NORMAN FRIEDMAN

CONTENTS

e. e. cummings

THE GROWTH OF A WRITER

1 INTRODUCTION

I WANT IN THIS BOOK to trace the development of Cummings as a writer. But "development" implies purposefulness, a goal toward which growth aims, and so I must begin at the end by trying to explain the meaning and significance of his mature work. Once this is done, we may proceed chronologically work by work, looking in each for signs of things to come—and, correspondingly, noting their absence. In this way, we will emerge with a synoptic view of the unfolding of a poet's career, which in Cummings' case should prove especially useful in view of the fact that he has often been accused of not growing up.

What significance we attribute to his mature work will of course depend upon what we take its meaning to be. By the "meaning" of his work I refer to the relationship between what Cummings is trying to do (his means) and why (his ends)—between his techniques on the one hand, and his attitudes and vision of life on the other. And it sometimes seems to me that no modern poet has been so persistently misunderstood merely on this level as has Cummings. Although I am certainly not alone in regarding him as a serious poet, a common view still has it that he is a curious mixture of naughty-boy anarchist and Cavalier love poet, with a penchant for scattering type across the page and using nothing but lower-case letters. Those who favor or disfavor him on this basis are both missing the real point: that lyric and satire play a functional role in a serious view of life, and that experimental techniques cannot be understood—much less evaluated—apart from that relationship. We must turn, then, to a discussion of his vision before going on to explain the meaning of his art.

i

One of the central insights embodied in literature, and especially in modern literature, is the sense that reality exceeds the forms which man has devised for dealing with it. Systems, codes, and theories are always being threatened by what they have excluded; reality, like a wolf, when denied entrance at the door, tries to climb down the chimney. It is true, however, that we sometimes become so used to unreality that we can scarcely tell the difference, as when our society makes a virtue of acquisitiveness, for example, and a vice of pleasure. But a man is not a man until he can understand the difference, and a writer is not a writer until he finds a language for expressing this understanding. There is always more to learning than books, there is always more to love than marriage, there is always more to work than a job, and there is always more to culture than civilization. And it is with this "more" that many nineteenth- and twentieth-century authors have been concerned.

Let us, for the sake of getting Cummings' vision of life into clearer focus, define four possible attitudes which one can take to this "more." There is first of all the Philistine, who fears reality and consequently wants to strengthen the forms. For him, life is dangerous and in need of control. Very few literary examples of this type come to mind, but perhaps Herman Wouk or James Gould Cozzens will serve. There is secondly, and at the opposite extreme, the Anarchist, who feels that the forms are killing us and consequently wants to free life altogether from their icy grip. Perhaps Henry Miller is an example of this type, but I'm not sure that's all he is. Then there is, thirdly, the Reformer, who realizes life contains more possibilities than our forms allow and consequently wants to make them more flexible. Dickens is an example of this type. And there is, finally, the Utopian, who wants to abolish the old forms in order to make new ones and so get more of the reality into them. George Bernard Shaw is an example of this type.

But this scheme is much too simple, much too didactic. There are so many writers who take a more complex view, who believe that one extreme can only be reached by going to the other. And Cummings is one of these. Let us define a few more types, then. Regarding the extremes, there are the Paradoxers, those who say that freedom is achieved through order, and those who say that order is achieved through freedom. For the first, renunciation leads to salvation, and Hopkins is one of these. For the second, there is a natural order which can only be achieved by discarding the artificial orders which man is always trying to impose upon it, and Blake, Coleridge, and Wordsworth are of this type. Regarding the more intermediate positions, there are the Ambivalents, those who choose the orderly while loving the free, as Captain Vere does in Melville's *Billy Budd*, and those who choose the free while loving the orderly, as does Aschenbach in Mann's *Death in Venice*.

Cummings belongs with Coleridge and the Romantic tradition in seeing the natural order as superior to man-made orders. He, like Coleridge, views nature as process rather than product, as dynamic rather than static, as organic rather than artificial, and as becoming rather than being. And he, like Coleridge, believes that the intuitive or imaginative faculty in man can perceive this *natura naturans* directly, and so he is a transcendentalist. Specifically, he believes there is a world of awareness—the true world—which is outside of, above, and beyond the ordinary world of everyday perception. The ordinary world is a world of habit, routine, and abstract categories, and hence lies like a distorting film over the true world of spontaneity, surprise, and concrete life. The ordinary world is a world of two-dimensional surfaces, facts, and nouns—it is a second-hand world. The true world is a world of three-dimensional depths, truths, and verbs—it is the first-hand world. For Cummings, it is the poet's function to decry the ordinary world and exalt the true, to represent not what any camera can see but to imitate the "actual crisp organic squirm" itself ("Gaston Lachaise," *Miscellany*, p. 29—see Bibliographical Note at end of book for key to references). Cummings' transcendental vision, then, is of a spiritual world, a world where facts are saturated in values, a world of magic, miracle, and mystery. Nothing which is merely measurable is for him of the slightest significance.

Now there are several misconceptions about such a vision which need to be cleared away. Yvor Winters, for example, holds that the Romantic view represents an abandonment to impulse and disorder, but this is completely to ignore the Romantic metaphysic. If one regards the intuitively perceived world as having a natural order of its own, then an attempt to grasp it represents not an abandonment to disorder but rather a struggle to realize a higher order. But Winters, I suspect, is simply a very sophisticated Philistine who takes the Romantics as Anarchists.

Another misconception is that the transcendentalist vision is in reality too simple, that it fails to do justice to both worlds. The ambivalence of Yeats, for example, is a case in point. In one poem he yearns for an escape from the ordinary world, and yet in another he vows allegiance to it. His work is shot through with the tension of trying to sustain a balance, and when he achieves transcendence, as at the end of "Dialogue of Self and Soul," it has been earned.

It is true, of course, that there is more passionate turmoil and self-doubt in the poems of Yeats than in those of Cummings, for Cummings begins, as it were, where Yeats leaves off. And it is true that many contemporary critics can say with a certain show of plausibility that Yeats's vision is more tragic, more noble, more mature. It is also true, however, that these differences could be taken to imply a difference in kind rather than of quality. Without for a moment suggesting that Yeats is not a great poet, can

we not suggest that he and Cummings are attempting
different things? For he is an Ambivalent while Cummings
is a Paradoxer.

There is no need to ask a Paradoxer to be an Ambivalent, nor should we criticize a freedom-Paradoxer for not
being a discipline-Paradoxer. It is, however, easy to confuse Cummings with the Anarchists and I myself have
been in the habit of postulating too clean a break in his
work between the ordinary and the transcendent worlds. I
see now, though, that their relationship is more complex
than I had thought. It is, first of all, a discipline to achieve
transcendent insight, and here is where the two sorts of
Paradoxers meet. For both, renunciation brings salvation,
surrender brings freedom—except for the discipline-
Paradoxer it is freedom which is surrendered, while for the
freedom-Paradoxer it is the ordinary world which is surrendered. What Cummings would have us renounce is not
our intuitive life but rather our desire for security, for
success, for stability, for comfort. And for most of us, this
would be a struggle indeed.

There is, furthermore, the mystery that the spiritual
ideal needs the ordinary world as an arena in which to
fulfill itself. Not only does love transform unlove; it needs
that unlove in order to come into being. In fact, the more
powerful the ordinary world happens to be, the more
this living ideal becomes itself. This paradox is what
Cummings calls "the ultimate meaning of existence,"
"The truth of truths" ("A Foreword to Krazy," *Miscellany*,
pp. 102–6). And it explains such phrases as "All lose,-
whole find" (a398, no. XVI), and "the most who die,the
more we live" (a401, no XX). May we not say, then,
that for Cummings the transcendental world, although
outside of, above, and beyond the ordinary world, is
vitally connected with that ordinary world, and indeed
depends upon it for its very existence?

But a third objection is not so easy to meet. It can be
said that in many poems the unlove of the ordinary world
is not transformed but rather hated. It is one thing to
decry false values and another to hate those who hold

them, and sometimes it seems that Cummings is too good a hater, turning even in the midst of a love poem to pour scorn on nonlovers. He himself has cited with great approval the passage in the New Testament where Christ forgives the woman taken in adultery (*i:six non-lectures*, pp. 66–67), and consistency with his own doctrine of transformation would require that his castigations of "mostpeople" be tempered with love. There is some evidence that they are so tempered, but there is too much evidence on the other side. Too often, when a brick hits this Krazy Kat the result is not love but rage. Perhaps this is because the one throwing it is Offissa Pupp (Society) rather than Ignatz Mouse (the individual). And for Cummings the mob is a gang, and so is not to be treated as if it were human. But the fact remains that there is a bit more spiteful peevishness and defensive boasting than we could wish in a poet who has a world of love to offer. I take this to be his main weakness and I want to face it honestly, not so that his detractors may have ammunition but so that they may come to see his flaws in the broader context of his strengths.

Let us conclude this section, then, by summing up Cummings' mature transcendental vision. This may be done under four related headings: the nature of the true world, knowing it, acting in it, and depicting it. Technically, these refer to his metaphysic, his epistemology, his politics, and his aesthetic. The true world, to begin with, is for him the natural world, the world of natural cyclical process. It is, furthermore, a timeless world of the eternal present—not that Cummings denies the past and the future, but rather that he denies that hope or regret, fear or nostalgia should usurp the living moment. This is a mystic concept, even a Zen concept, but it can be explained in simple terms: since time involves the sense of sequence, you are living in the world of timelessness when you eliminate your consciousness of sequence— when you destroy, that is, the memories and hopes which would distract you from what is happening in the moment. Thus is it that to live purely in the here and now is to live in the timeless world. The true world is, finally, an actual world, and paradoxically, a world of the dream. I think Cummings intends by this to mean that it is a world of imagination, of our deeper selves. And the opposite or ordinary world is, contrariwise, the artificial world, the world of time, and the merely real or logical world.

How do we know the true world? Here Cummings is not so much antirational as he is nonrational. Knowledge, which is rational and belongs to the ordinary world, is the same thing as unlearning ignorance. But it is not wisdom, for wisdom, like love, is a spiritual gift: not fact but truth is the goal. Now there's nothing wrong with knowledge —except when it's confused with wisdom. And, indeed, the most rational man must admit—and if he doesn't, he's hardly being rational in committing what Whitehead has called the fallacy of misplaced concreteness—that there is an area of ultimate values which lies beyond our logic. Logic itself, like geometry, rests upon axioms which cannot be proved; the physicist in his laboratory cannot simply gather data, for he must frame hypotheses and make assumptions in order to make any sense out of these data. How much more so is it in the practical field of human actions that unprovable first assumptions lie behind everything. And it is here, where desire and will rather than reason and proof are the determining factors, that Cummings lives. Moral choice is based on the ultimate image we have of what we are and want to become, a commitment rather than a demonstration. Values are the basis of logic rather than its product. And in order to "know" them we must get out of the categories and dare to face ultimates directly, intuitively, and spontaneously.

Cummings' politics may be summed up in two words— love, and the individual. Let us consider the individual first. Since truth can only be grasped intuitively at first hand, it follows that one cannot get it from others but must experience it for himself. If one is to "know" at first hand, it follows that one must live at first hand, refusing to be dominated by one's institutional and societal roles. One must live directly and spontaneously, freely and responsively. Hence the individual is a lover, an artist, a tramp, a clown—even an adolescent, for the adolescent has not yet been integrated into society—anyone who has managed to escape the categories. Now the problem is that Cummings seems to have no sense of community, of how people can be more than just individuals and live creatively together. For him, all groups of more than two are gangs, and collectivism of any kind—fascist, communist, socialist, liberal—is anathema. Only the personal is real, and happiness can happen only to people. Institutions can harm us, or they can at best enable us, but they cannot give us what we want. Thus, for the individual, "all/ history is too small," and for lovers, "exceedingly too small" (a412, no. XXXIX).

What may be said in defense of this attitude? That in criticizing society he is addressing himself to actual societies and not to an ideal community? Well, yes: this explains a lot. The police state is the prime fact of our time, and it's hard to believe that one can say too much against it—wherever it may be found and under whatever guise. But Cummings is not a Reformer or a Utopian, and he has no institutions to suggest in place of those he criticizes. A defense, however, can be built in favor of the Anarchist, even if Cummings is not simply an Anarchist. He takes his stand from a point outside our world, and we need him if only for the perspective on ourselves which he affords us. Material progress and welfare are simply not part of his scheme of values, since they belong to the world of fact and knowledge rather than of truth and wisdom. He warns us continually not to take means as ends, and all his emphasis is on the side of ends.

And what of ends? What he calls love is the answer, and he intends by this more than erotic romance, although this is certainly a part of it. What he means by love is simply perfect givingness, giving without thought of return, illimitably and openly and freely. As he says in his essay on Krazy Kat, love hasn't a why or because or although; there are no conditions, no strings attached. And because only a person who has achieved perfect selfhood can give freely, only a true individual can love. On the other hand, when a person has no faith in himself, he needs someone else's love to give him this faith, and so he gives his love in return for this faith. But since his need for security is bottomless, his need for love becomes insatiable and he sucks the life out of his beloved (something like this was troubling D. H. Lawrence, was it not?). The beloved is being asked to do for him what he can't do for himself: she is being asked to give over her soul, and this is a desire for power and not love. So self-sacrifice becomes one more way of gaining power over someone: give to me because I have given, repay me in kind. And love degenerates into a power-struggle, one manipulating the other for the sake of his own need, his weapon disguised under unimpeachable banners. But real love makes no demands, asks for no rewards, does not seek for control, and covets no possession. It is not something you acquire, like property, and the beloved is not something you own.

And what is love's relation to society and the individual? The individual, tending to be naturally selfish, tries to destroy love. Society, tending to be institutionally altruistic, tries to protect love by restraining the individual. Although neither of them understand her, she fulfills herself only when society fails to suppress the individual. It is his hate which she transforms, and his hate is intensified by the collectivist benevolence of society. The individual needs society, therefore, just as love needs the individual. Out of this struggle the ideal is born. Cummings seems to envision a society, then, in which love is realized out of the dialectic play between the Anarchist and the Philistine. Its essential condition is freedom, for if there were no individuals left no one would ever have any genuine feelings again. The role of the Philistine seems to be essentially negative: he exists to be thwarted, but his existence is essential to the individual as a spur. And he is attacked by Cummings when he is too successful. It is useless, then, to try to put a label on Cummings' politics: he is neither a liberal nor a reactionary, neither a Democrat nor a Republican.

The view of art which follows from this metaphysic, this epistemology, and these politics is, accordingly, Romantic. Art imitates nature, and since nature is dynamic, spontaneous, and concrete, art tries to achieve the miracle of the verb rather than the deadness of the noun. A poem should not be *about* something, it should *be* something. Nor does this imply an anarchistic abandonment of intelligence, and those wild men are mistaken who believe that poetry is written "spontaneously" without thought or care. Cummings is one of the most painstaking of craftsmen. Intelligence, for him, is essential, but it is "intelligence functioning at intuitional velocity" ("Gaston Lachaise," *Miscellany*, p. 27). A truly primitive view is not self-consciously childish, for it requires of us "an intelligent process of the highest order, namely the negation on our part, by thinking, of thinking"—it does not deny the intelligence but rather digests it (p. 28). And this brings us to a consideration of Cummings' own art, of the means used to achieve these ends and embody these attitudes.

ii

Technically and stylistically, we would expect Cummings, in view of all that has been said, to be unconventional, an experimentalist. But here again we must not forget that we are dealing with a Paradoxer or we will miss the large and essential body of tradition in which he works. And not merely the obvious traditions of rhyme and meter—and even here how often does the common view fail to notice his sonnets and his quatrains—but also the more subtle tonalities of the Elizabethan song, the eighteenth-century satire, the nineteenth-century lyric, the remembrances of Campion, Jack Donne, Dryden, Blake, Wordsworth, Keats, Emerson, Whitman, Dickinson, and Thoreau. In being unconventional, Cummings is not being antiliterary. He was an educated man, and spoke with pride of his Latin and Greek. It is equally mistaken to be surprised at the catholicity and traditionalism of his literary tastes as it is to be amazed that a naughty-boy satirist can be a cavalier love lyrist. These are contradictions only to those who have tried to put Cummings in too narrow a category to begin with.

But his technical innovations are many and spectacular. Not anarchistic flauntings of sense, they are best understood as various ways of stripping the film of familiarity from language in order to strip the film of familiarity from the world. Transform the word, he seems to have felt, and you are on the way to transforming the world. Cummings' technical and stylistic devices are means of unlocking the kernels of aliveness within the husks of convention. I once said that the quality of his work should be defined in term of modernist techniques for approaching traditional subjects, and one critic took this as evidence for concluding that Cummings has nothing new to say and so must wrap it up in gaudy packages to make it appear new. This inference can make one despair of reviewers, for I said "subjects" and not "insights"—but let that pass. The real problem here is the assumption that the worth of a poet is somehow directly connected with the newness of what he has to say. But surely it is a respectable theory which holds that the poet's function is to make us *realize* what we already know. And isn't it also plausible that the *way* something is said somehow alters *what* is said, or at least gives it its particular meaning vis-à-vis the reader? I am sure, for example, that the explanation I have given of Cummings' vision, although I hope it is informative, is hardly moving, however new that vision might be. It is the poet's job not so much to *have* a vision of the world as it is to touch it into life for us. What Keats said about truth being tested on the pulses applies here, and what happened to Shaw's English Chaplain after he saw Saint Joan burn at the stake illustrates the point. In our own experience we can hardly "know" something until we have *felt* it somehow; so too in poetry the poet must make us feel what he is saying before we can understand it.

And that is where his technical and stylistic devices come in. I leave it to the reader to judge whether what Cummings has to say is "new" or not—although I doubt whether it can be said too often—and concern myself with the ways in which he attempts to make us feel it. Language is a two-edged weapon: it clarifies our experience for us and helps us master and extend our world, but at the same time it removes us from the very reality we are attempting to come to grips with. I refer the reader to Muir's "The Animals," Graves's "The Cool Web," and Auden's "Their Lonely Betters." And both of these effects are products of the same cause, namely the abstracting and systematizing powers of language. Language cannot serve its purposes without conventions, but it can also serve these purposes only too well. The all-too-frequent result is sterility, deadness, and lack of felt significance. Words become counters to be manipulated instead of seeds of meaning. Anyone familiar with modern criticism will immediately recognize T. E. Hulme and Ezra Pound behind this paragraph, and hence will recognize that the problems faced by Cummings are those faced by most modernist writers: how to reverse the drag of language toward deadness without losing intelligibility altogether; how to "make it new" without destroying it.

Clearly, the answer is that they must somehow distort the normal conventions without breaking them, and paradoxically they must face the problem afresh every time one of these distortions becomes a convention in its turn. And, indeed, most experimenters must acknowledge inevitable failure at the outset, for if they succeed in establishing an innovation on an intelligible basis so that it does communicate, then it is more than likely that both they and their readers will begin responding to it automatically and without feeling. Thus does manner deteriorate into mannerism. Nor has Cummings escaped this fate. And who has?—Eliot, Pound, Stevens, Auden, Frost?

But this is a relative matter. Very few poets can remake themselves three times over as Yeats did. It is enough for a poet to create one genuine innovation in a lifetime, even if he doesn't go beyond it himself. And, I might say, even if it never succeeds in influencing anyone else: it is another curious doctrine that a poet's value is somehow directly related to his influence, as if bad poets don't influence others, or as if good poets don't have a bad influence. It is enough for a poet to devise one way of making us see one truth, and no amount of repetition can undo this good work once it has been achieved. This Cummings has done—and more. Although some of his early poetry is wild with typographical distortions, and some of his middle and later poetry is clogged with his own peculiarly twisted diction and syntax, it is not true that he doesn't grow and develop—in these as in other matters. Sometimes he repeats himself, sometimes his devices fall into place with a mechanical regularity, and sometimes his oddness is tiresome. But any experimenter by definition takes more chances than the ordinary writer: so long as he wins more often than he loses, his failures are worthwhile. This Cummings has done—and more. When he wins, he wins like no one else: his best poems are of such a miraculous purity, so precise a feeling, so fresh a vision, that he can be forgiven his losses. His growth represents not so much the perfection and abandonment of one device after another as the gradual discovery and mastery of a group of devices. Those who see no growth here have simply not troubled to look.

And what are these devices? Where Hulme and others found their answer in the miracle of metaphor, Cummings found his chiefly in the magic of the word itself. Concerned less with the interplay of ambiguities than with the vitalizing of movement, he has coined a vocabulary in which nouns are made out of verbs, thus preserving sense while at the same time creating motion. The knife-grinder who "sharpens say to sing" (a443, no. 26) is also a poet who puts a keen edge on words. By means of this grammatical shift, the word has a noun husk but a verb kernel—what is needed is a noun, but what is meant is a verb. Not merely is there an aesthetic pleasure here in recognizing old friends in new disguises; there is also a significant insight produced as the reader makes the connection in his mind between meaning and function, between content and form. And this insight is that the mind can only grasp the truth of what is being said by means of motion. As the mind moves back and forth between the recognition that this is a noun and the discovery that it was once a verb, somewhere along the arc of insight it perceives the truth of what is being said: that the knife-grinder achieves a mystery of transformation in turning prose into poetry—he "sharpens say to sing." The mind perceives this because it has been asked to participate in the very process of transformation itself. This must be what Cummings means when he says that art is not *of* something, but rather *is* something; it imitates nature, and the reader becomes not a passive spectator but an active protagonist. The grammatical shift imitates the meaning, and in the resultant interplay something like a metaphor is produced—except that the two terms are not tenor and vehicle but rather noun-function and verb-meaning. Laborious analysis, however, should not obscure the rapidity, the delicacy, and the delight with which the reader senses all this.

Nouns are also made out of prefixes, interrogative pronouns, conjunctions, and so on. Similarly, coinages are created by analogy by adding adverbial suffixes where you least expect them ("happeningly"), adjectival suffixes ("neverish"), and noun-endings ("muchness"). These are Cummings' true trademarks, the devices the critics, imitators, and parodists are bound to miss in their anxiety to fasten upon the more obvious typographical pyrotechnics. Also more characteristic are his distortions of syntax, and these too are missed by the readers who run.

But the typography deserves discussion. I, for one, like it in most instances; it seems to me just, useful, and right. But I recognize the possibility that I may simply be used to it. I also recognize the force of the argument which says these devices are not organic or functional because they can rarely be pronounced. And I understand furthermore that they often succeed in irritating people. Let me try, however, to say what can be said for them.

To break lines and words on the page, to use capitals and lower case letters where they don't belong, to insert

parentheses anywhere and everywhere, to scatter punctuation marks apparently at random—what uses can these
serve? There is, first of all, what I suspect is a heuristic
function for the poet: it was simply helpful for Cummings
to do these things as he tried to write a poem. And as
such, we should be willing to accept them. But, of course,
we could argue that he might just as well have gotten rid
of them after the poem was written. So let us look for
better reasons. There is, secondly, the "feel" of the poem
as it lies on the page. To me at least there is a pleasurable
tactility in these devices, a sense of visual structure as in a
painting. Does not a reader of conventional poetry take a
similar pleasure in the look of a sonnet or of a blank verse
paragraph? This may have nothing to do with the meaning
involved, but it is present and affective nevertheless. The
third is the best reason, for it is here that the charge
of inorganicity can be met: typography may not be pro-
nounceable but it does affect the way we read. Pause and
emphasis are supported by these devices; the meaning of
words and lines is underscored; but, most importantly of
all, meanings are created as the reader's mind is slowed in
its progress through the poem and forced to go back and
forth, thereby becoming aware of the meanings in an immediate moment of perception. This is what any good
poem asks of the reader and Cummings is simply extend-
ing this request by making it explicit. Nor is it necessary
to scorn a device which enables the poet to get two words
for the price of one, as Cummings does, for example,
when he splits "nowhere" into "now" and "here" (b, no.
4). When he said he was fond of that precision which
creates movement (Foreword to *is* 5, a163) he was in fact
announcing the fundamental tenet of his aesthetic.

iii

To explain the meaning of Cummings' work—to
show the relationship between his devices and the vision
they serve—is in a sense to meet one charge regarding its
significance. For it is not uncommonly said that there is no
meaning here and that therefore there is no significance. I

would feel that the present book had achieved its purpose if this one point were to be finally recognized by all those who are concerned with modern poetry: that Cummings' experiments, his love poems, and his satires all play a functional role in a serious view of life—or, at least, a *view* of life, for its seriousness must be discussed separately. No one can honestly read these poems and conclude that Cummings is a trifler; no one can honestly read this book and say that Cummings' poetry has no meaning. A Campion, a Herrick, a Prior, a Landor, a Dowson may be consummate artists, and we may cherish them for their perfection of style and language, but a case can reasonably be made against them for not having anything much to say. Not necessarily anything *new* to say, but anything *much* to say. Cummings, however, is not one of these.

But it's the seriousness of his vision which, even if it be admitted to exist, may be questioned. Well, I have already discussed what may be said against it and have tried to answer certain objections. Cummings' view of life is nonrational, and he sometimes sees himself as the Fool, the Outcast, the Clown, and so on, vis-à-vis ordinary society. He is more interested, as Walter Pater was, in experiencing life than in theorizing about it, but for a rather different reason—Pater's moments of crystallization were precious because nature is always dying, while Cummings' are precious because nature is always just being born. He is interested in what is alive and growing, in what is therefore immeasurable and mysterious. Now there always have been and there always will be those who disagree with this attitude, and that is their privilege. But this is no necessary reason to discount its value as a serious poetic vision; indeed, it may be claimed that it is *the* poetic vision of most great literature since Blake, if not earlier. It has, at least, a certifiable literary history. And I for one think no truly rational man will deny the importance of a nonrational view of certain aspects of life—those in which Cummings is most interested.

It is unfortunate, however, that as many Romantics have misprized reason as there have been Rationalists who have misprized the imagination, and Cummings has not avoided this error. Nor has he avoided the error of demolishing all institutions in his anxiety to attack the evil ones which are still sucking the life out of us. But he may be defended against both charges on the grounds that his destructive work is needed and is therefore healthy, for there are times when going to extremes is required by the extremity of the evil to be corrected. And these are extreme times indeed: most of what he attacks has gotten worse instead of better during the course of his lifetime; and more and more, recent history is proving him right about what's wrong with the world.

Of course, one may have a serious view of life and still not be a significant poet. So the question must also be discussed as to whether Cummings' means are suitable to embody his ends—suitable, that is, in relation to what other poets have done regarding similar ends. For I hope I have already shown that his means are appropriate as ways of creating the freshness and motion and vitality which his vision calls for. If we ask of a poet that he not merely achieve his goal but also that he achieve it in an original and unexpected way, then Cummings fills the bill. There is nothing tame, nothing passive, nothing easy about his solution of his artistic problems: he is an innovator, an experimenter, a questioner. It is of the essence in the transcendental view never to rest content with any formulation of life's truth for long, and so it is necessary that transcendentalist writers be odd, cranky, even perverse. It is nonsense, therefore, to complain that Cummings hasn't influenced anyone—even if this were true.

We also have the right to expect of a poet that he know and revere the traditions of his art even as he is violating them. If Cummings says "welcome the future," he also says "honour the past" (b, no. 60). He knows there is nothing which is merely new; he knows and understands more about language and its responsibilities, I suspect, than the critics who have complained of his whimsicality and arbitrariness. If my first point in this book is that Cummings has a serious vision of life, my second point is that both it and his art are firmly rooted in tradition. No artistic experimenter can be significant who is not so rooted.

Or, it may be agreed that all I have said about Cummings is so, but that other transcendentalist poets—or at least poets whose view of life is framed by spiritual or imaginative insights—have done it better. I have tried to explain this point by distinguishing between the Paradoxers and the Ambivalents, and by suggesting that we need not limit our appreciation to the Ambivalents. Why not? The Ambivalents are characterized by self-doubt, and Cummings is surely not one of these. When they achieve a joyful moment of release, it is always at the end of their poems; Cummings begins where they leave off. In Aristotelian terms, their personae are people like us, while Cummings' persona is one who is better than we are. Theirs is an art of struggle, his of achievement. Naturally theirs is more flattering to us, his less. But does not their art encourage complacency in us, especially when it is written by the fashionable imitators whose ambivalence is a literary pose rather than a felt experience? As if to say that joy is a remote thing and we are in the swim if we feel despair. How much more difficult it is to write a really affirmative piece—more difficult than one would suppose —for it is so much harder to fake. False enthusiasm is easier by far to spot than false gloom. The value of Cummings' stance is in part a function of its rarity in twentieth-century poetry.

An interesting light is thrown on these remarks by Cummings himself, in a letter to Allen Tate, which I saw only after completing this chapter (Mr. Tate informs me that he thinks the "self portrait" refers to an early draft of his poem, "The Eye," which he wrote in 1947):

Dear Allen—
I am deeply touched by the self portrait
(enclosed herewith) which you were so
generous as to loan me. But (this is
my own perfectly biased opinion)
tu as tort in one respect: he who

serves La De'esse Qui s'apelle "l'art"
hath luck beyond rubrics n + 3 . . .
Whereas (I feel) you've almost
pretendedyourself into sadness-extraneous,
tristesse-irrelevant, and grief-worldly.
Bien sûr, l'existence est difficile
(et comment!) for each him who
desires La Vie; quite as difficile
as it's facile for all unartists.

Having described the meaning and significance of the mature work, I want now to track Cummings' development as he grows toward and fulfills that maturity. We will proceed, as a matter of convenience, by decades, and so we turn to the first decade, the 1920's.

CUMMINGS' FIRST BOOK was preceded by a scattering of poems and essays in various periodicals. For the sake of convenience, I plan to discuss only those poems which appeared in book form, and these will be taken up in the next chapter. A brief examination of three of the essays here, however, will serve to launch our analysis of *The Enormous Room.*

"The New Art" (*Miscellany*, pp. 17–22), which was a commencement address on the occasion of his graduation from Harvard in 1915, was published in *The Harvard Advocate*, June 1915. And it is peculiarly fitting that Cummings should have begun his career by defending Cubism and Futurism in painting; the new music of Franck, Debussy, Ravel, and Satie; and the literary experiments of Amy Lowell, Donald Evans, and Gertrude Stein (although he had his doubts in the latter case). But it is also especially significant that his thesis should be that the new art represented "a clearly discernable evolution from models," "a natural unfolding of sound tendencies." His view of experimentation, then, is clearly set within the framework of tradition, and he finds that the new art contains no "trace of that abnormality, or incoherence, which the casual critic is fond of making the subject of tirades against the new order."

Some five years later, after he had returned from the experiences recorded in *The Enormous Room*, certain of his values were becoming clearer. The essays on Gaston

Lachaise (*Miscellany*, pp. 23–33) and T. S. Eliot (*ibid.*, pp. 34–37) both appeared in *The Dial* in 1920. The first is especially important for his exposition of the organic view of nature as opposed to the adult world of habit and stereotype, for it is here that the first signs of his transcendentalism make their appearance. What is really interesting is the length of time it took for this vision to flower into poetry. As we shall see, there are important signs of it in *The Enormous Room* and in *Him* (1927), but it took this entire first decade for Cummings to mature sufficiently to have this vision leave any palpable mark in his poems. Of course, the conception of nature in his early poems is implicitly organic in the way he stresses movement and kinesis in his descriptions, but this is not the same thing as using such a conception as a value principle. For I do not find any explicit transcendentalism in his poetry until *ViVa* (1931), his fourth volume of poems and his eighth published book.

The essay on Eliot is chiefly remarkable for Cummings' immediate recognition of the value of Eliot's early work, and for his insistence that the function of art is to assert a fresh and individual vision. "By technique," he says, "we do mean one thing: the alert hatred of normality which, through the lips of a tactile and cohesive adventure, asserts that nobody in general and someone in particular is incorrigibly and actually alive. This someone is, it would seem, the extremely great artist: or, he who prefers above everything and within everything the unique dimension of intensity, which it amuses him to substitute in us for the comforting and comfortable furniture of reality." Let us turn now to *The Enormous Room*.

i

This book is devoted, as he says, to "recalling (in God knows a rather clumsy and perfectly inadequate way) what happened to me between the latter part of August 1917 and the first day of January 1918" (p. 313). What happened to him was that he was thrown into a French prison, or rather "a *Porte* or *Camp de Triage*," a place where suspicious persons were detained until their guilt or innocence was decided upon by a Commission which visited La Ferté Macé once every three months (p. 83). The place where the sixty men lived under the most primitive conditions, was the "enormous room," "in shape oblong, about 80 feet by 40, unmistakably ecclesiastical in feeling—two rows of wooden pillars, spaced at intervals of fifteen feet, rose to a vaulted ceiling 25 or 30 feet above the floor" (p. 70). It was, in effect, a concentration camp, the symbol of the modern police state. And it was here that Cummings experienced for himself, at the age of 23, the disease of modern civilization.

Not that he hadn't started out with high hopes, for he had enlisted in the Norton-Harjes Ambulance Corps before the United States entered the war. His troubles had to do, significantly, with censorship, and, just as significantly, at second remove, for his was probably the first recorded case of guilt by association. It appears that Slater Brown, his close friend in the Corps, had written some letters back home which were critical of the French government and its war effort (see Norman, pp. 91–95), and that these had been intercepted by the French authorities. Both were thereupon put into custody, Cummings on the grounds that he was Brown's friend: "we were always together and . . . consequently I might properly be regarded as a suspicious character" (p. 16).

But the remarkable thing and, as we shall see, the clue to the book's meaning, is the fact that they both were glad to leave the Corps and go to jail. Imprisonment was for them, in spite of the suffering involved, a release. Cummings concludes, at the end of the book, that "I have proved to my own satisfaction . . . that I was happier in La Ferté Macé . . . than the very keenest words can pretend to express" (p. 313). Part of the reason is found in the nature of their life at *section sanitaire* of the Corps where they were stationed, or rather in the nature of their chief. "The doughy face. Imitation-English-officer swagger. Large calves, squeaking puttees. The daily lecture: . . . We gotta show these lousy Frenchmen what Americans are. We gotta show we're superior to 'em. Those bastards doughno what a bath means" (64–65). The trouble was that Cummings and Brown wanted to fraternize with the natives and their chief was down on them for this. Well, they got their wish! And that is the other part of the reason, for in prison they discovered the mystery of the individual.

The book has thirteen chapters, and these fall naturally into four groups. Chapters I–IV serve to bring Cummings to La Ferté Macé; Chapters V–VII describe the life and the people there; Chapters VIII–XI are reserved for a treatment of four very special inmates, the Delectable Mountains; and Chapters XII–XIII tell of his release and return to America. I will summarize briefly the contents of each of these groups of chapters in turn.

He begins his "pilgrimage" in Chapter I. Having served almost three of their six months' term in the Corps, Cummings and Brown are taken separately from their station to see Monsieur le Ministre de Sûreté de Noyon. Not knowing why or where he is being taken, Cummings experiences the thrill "of being yanked from the putrescent banalities of an official non-existence into a high and clear adventure" (p. 7). At Noyon he is fed and put into a cell. Then he is interrogated by Monsieur le Ministre and discovers what the trouble is. He is given a chance to free himself when he is asked whether he hates the Germans. He answers instead, "Non. J'aime beaucoup les français," and thereby seals his fate as a criminal (p. 19). In Chapter II he is en route to prison, being taken by train to a small jail where he sleeps a while. He is back on the train in Chapter III, and arrives with his captors in Paris. There they wait for the train to "Mah-say," which Cummings mistakenly takes to be Marseilles. They disembark at Briouse and walk at night to their final destination. In Chapter IV he finds himself in the enormous room, meets Brown there, and realizes at last where he is. He becomes familiar with his surroundings and fellow inmates, and learns the routine of the place. He is interrogated once again.

Now the special quality of this first part of the book is

Cummings' mounting gaiety in the face of his increasing physical discomfort. During this time he has gotten dirtier and tireder than he has ever been, and yet he says, at the end of the fourth chapter, "I reclined in an ecstasy of happiness and weariness. There could be nothing better than this. To sleep" (p. 112). The point is, as the opening of the next chapter indicates, that he is experiencing the sense of release one feels when he has nothing left to lose or hope for. And this became, as we shall see, one of the central experiences of his life. Throughout this part, indeed, I seem to sense dim foreshadowings of Camus' *The Stranger*.

In Chapter V we have an explicit transition, for Cummings switches from a chronological narration to an exposition of the people and the place. Here he tells of the various reasons why certain of the prisoners are confined at La Ferté Macé. As one might expect in the case of political arrest, these reasons are vague and ambiguous. One could be put in jail simply for being in the wrong place at the wrong time, for being of the wrong nationality, for having the wrong opinions, or simply for looking suspicious. As he recounts these stories, Cummings wonders what the great and good French Government could have to fear from this mixed bag of helpless and harmless people. And he learns what can happen to people when they are thrust into prison, how their essential cruelty or essential humanity emerges under stress. In Chapter VI he describes Monsieur le Directeur and the instruments of his power—Fear, Women, and Sunday. Here Cummings learns the nature of bureaucracy, how people are managed and controlled. Naturally, his contempt for the guards and the police is bottomless. And he learns also that women are not necessarily the weaker sex, for he tells of the brutality which some of them endured (women prisoners, of course, had their own separate enormous room at La Ferté). Chapter VII tells of the various inmates who arrived after Cummings did, and serves as a prelude to the next part.

There are four Delectable Mountains, or supremely human beings, and Cummings devotes a chapter to each of them. The first is Joseph Demestre, a gypsy called *The Wanderer*, whose wife and three children came and begged to be made prisoners too. The commission decided, in its infinite wisdom, upon learning he was not legally married to her, to confine him at another prison altogether, thereby separating the family and inflicting a perfectly gratuitous anguish upon all concerned. The second is Zoo-Loo, or Zulu, a gentle and generous Pole. The third is Surplice, a dirty, humble, utterly simple-minded person, who plays the fool to the scorn of the others—he considers it a compliment to be noticed, even with a curse. And the fourth is Jean Le Nègre, a great and gay childlike negro who had been arrested for impersonating an officer.

The final part brings Cummings home. In Chapter XII he is released, and in Chapter XIII he takes his leave and departs.

ii

And what is this book's central meaning, its governing conception? The answer may be approached by several stages. There is, first of all, the unity of the experience itself: it begins with Cummings' arrest, deals with the consequences of that incident, and concludes with his release. That is to say, although the structure is basically autobiographical, it so happens that this incident was organically complete in itself. All Cummings had to do, at least on the level of "plot," was to follow nature.

But clearly this is no mere adventure story, however interesting it may be in itself. It is not simply a bit of authentic history, either personal or historical. Furthermore, although our indignation is to be aroused against the organized and official mistreatment of human beings, this is no tract either. Cummings' central concern is not with injustice and how to alleviate it; this is not a diatribe against France, or against concentration camps, or against the war. As he says in the Introduction to the Modern Library Edition, written ten years after the book was first published, "When *The Enormous Room* was published, some people wanted a war book; they were disappointed."

What Cummings is really after is implied by the emotional tone of the book, the joy he feels when the individual triumphs over the system which has done its best to destroy him. This triumph is further suggested by the loose symbolic parallel Cummings uses, the parallel between this experience and Bunyan's *Pilgrim's Progress* which is contained in some of his chapter headings and terminology. The symbolism is that of the journey through suffering to a rebirth, a story of falling to rise, and that is the meaning of Cummings' "plot." Its culmination is the gradual discovery he makes, because of his imprisonment, of the mystery of the individual and of the timeless world. It is, in other words, the experience through which he first became confirmed in his transcendental vision. As he said thirty years later, in his summing up of *i:six nonlectures*, "So ends the last lesson of a nondivisible ignoramus: a double lesson—outwardly and inwardly affirming that, whereas a world rises to fall, a spirit descends to ascend" (p. 110).

And what is this mystery of the individual? "Then I saw in my Dream," Bunyan writes, "that on the morrow he got up to go forwards, but they desired him to stay till the next day also; and then, said they, we will (if the day be clear) show you the Delectable Mountains, which, they said, would yet further add to his comfort, because they were were nearer the desired Haven than the place where at present he was: so he consented and stayed. When the morning was up, they had him to the top of the House, and bid him look South; so he did: and behold at a great distance he saw a most pleasant Mountainous Country, beautified with Woods, Vineyards, Fruits of all sorts, Flowers also, with Springs and Fountains, very delectable to behold. Then he asked the name of the country:

"They said it was *Immanuel's Land*; and it is as common, they said, as this *Hill* is, to and for all the Pilgrims. And when thou comest there, from thence, said they,

thou mayest see to the gate of the Coelestial City, as
the Shepherds that live there will make appear" (Harvard
Classics edition, pp. 58–59).

Cummings, in trying vainly to describe one of his Delectable Mountains, says, "There are certain things in
which one is unable to believe for the simple reason that
he never ceases to feel them. Things of this sort—things
which are always inside of us and in fact are us and which
consequently will not be pushed off or away where we
can begin thinking about them—are no longer things;
they, and the us which they are, equals A Verb; an IS. The
Zulu, then, I must per force call an IS" (p. 231). In speaking of the genuinely primitive vision of the true artist, in
his essay on Lachaise, he says: "Consequently to appreciate child art we are compelled to undress one by one the
soggy nouns whose agglomeration constitutes the mechanism of Normality, and finally to liberate the actual crisp
organic squirm—the IS" (*Miscellany*, p. 29).

The individual, for Cummings, is an apotheosis, a revelation of the organic miracle of life, a vision of nature in
man which is salvation for the beholder, redeeming him
from the death of the stereotype into the life of the actual
and transcendent world. An individual, to put it—not
without loss—into ordinary terms, is a person who is
naturally and honestly responsive, who feels and sees truly
and apart from conventional categories. And this is the
mystery of his four Delectable Mountains. People, on the
other hand, who can live and respond only in terms of
those categories are not individuals, those whom Cummings comes to call "mostpeople" later on. Monsieur le
Ministre de Sûreté de Noyon, for example, who asks him
if he hates the Germans: when Cummings replies no,
that he loves the French, Monsieur le Ministre replies, "It
is impossible to love Frenchmen and not to hate Germans" (p. 19).

So, as Cummings learns the mystery of the individual,
he learns simultaneously the true meaning of civilization.
Speaking of one of his fellow inmates, who was jailed for
being a Socialist, he says: "After all, it is highly improbable

that this poor socialist suffered more at the hands of the
great and good American government; or—since all great
governments are *per se* good and vice versa—than did
many a man in general who was cursed with a talent for
thinking during the warlike moments recently passed;
during that is to say an epoch when the g. and g. nations
demanded of their respective peoples the exact antithesis
to thinking; said antithesis being vulgarly called Belief"
(p. 139). And a few pages later, he observes: "O gouverne-
ment français, I think it was not very clever of You to
put this terrible doll in La Ferté; I should have left him in
Belgium with his little doll-wife if I had been You; for
when Governments are found dead there is always a little
doll on top of them, pulling and tweaking with his
little hands to get back the microscopic knife which
sticks firmly in the quiet meat of their hearts" (p. 142).
Speaking, finally, of the terrible solitary confinement in-
flicted upon a tubercular woman prisoner, he says: "I
realized fully and irrevocably and for perhaps the first
time the meaning of civilization. And I realized that it
was true—as I had previously only suspected it to be true—
that in finding us unworthy of helping to carry forward
the banner of progress, alias the tricolour, the inimitable
and excellent French Government was conferring upon B.
and myself—albeit with other intent—the ultimate compliment" (p. 167).

And what is that ultimate compliment? Obviously, the
irony says it's better to be in jail with human beings than
in society with those who put those human beings into
jail. But there's more to it than that, for this "compliment"
becomes the way to salvation itself, and this is one
genuine sense in which Cummings is a Paradoxer. For
Cummings discovers that one escapes from the deadness
of society by enduring the worst it can inflict, and this is
a favor, a compliment indeed.

How does this happen? As we have seen, Cummings
shifts his method of presentation between Chapters
IV and V from chronological narration to static exposition.
The reason is that he loses, after his second day at La

Ferté, any sense of sequence; one day begins to look very much like the next, and as a result events occur and are remembered as "individualities distinct from Time itself" (pp. 113–14). Now this is a moment of supreme importance for Cummings and for those who would understand him: "the diary or time method is a technique which cannot possibly do justice to timelessness." He experiences "that actual Present—without future and past—whereof they alone are cognizant who, so to speak, have submitted to an amputation of the world." It is not simply that he is for the individual and against society, although I hope I have shown that this opposition came to him out of a significant experience and not simply out of crankiness or eccentricity. The truth of the matter is to be found in *why* he is for the individual and against society: because the one represents an actual world of spontaneous responsiveness while the other constitutes a dead world of sterile and often vicious habit. It's not so much the injustice and cruelty of society, then, which he opposes, as it is its lack of life.

But the central meaning of this book, and of Cummings' art as a whole, is to be found in the phrase, the "amputation of the world." It should be clear that he means the ordinary world, and the point is that his conception of the transcendent world involves a surrender, a surrender which is often induced by suffering—the joy aroused in Krazy Kat when she is struck by Ignatz' brick. One submits to the world's categories in order to transcend them; one needs to endure its cruelties in order to be shocked into life. For the ordinary world is by nature a habit, and it takes trouble to get out of a habit, trouble created when that habit itself becomes sufficiently outrageous. So it is a compliment to be sent to jail, a joy to become a prisoner, a blessing to be tortured.

His conception of art is therefore a function of his conception of the transcendent world. It is a world of the actual Present, and hence a world of timelessness. Past and future are the products of language, and language is abstract. The ordinary world is a colossal hoax of clocks and calendars, and the problem of art is to recover *through* language what language has helped to take away from us. Thus, as the prisoner gives up the ordinary world to experience timelessness through the suffering of confinement, so too does the artist give up his conventional box of tricks to create a living reality through the discipline of experiment. "There is and can be no such thing as authentic art," he says toward the end of *The Enormous Room*, "until the *bons trucs* (whereby we are taught to see and imitate on canvas and in stone and by words this so-called world) are entirely and thoroughly and perfectly annihilated by that vast and painful process of Unthinking which may result in a minute bit of purely personal Feeling. Which minute bit is Art" (p. 307). The phrasing is similar in his earlier essay on Lachaise: "But the inexcusable and spontaneous scribblings which children make on sidewalks, walls, anywhere, preferably with coloured chalk, cannot be grasped until we have accomplished the thorough destruction of the world. By this destruction alone we cease to be spectators of a ludicrous and ineffectual striving and, involving ourselves in a new and fundamental kinesis, become protagonist's of the child's vision" (*Miscellany*, p. 28).

But in spite of his emphasis upon amputation, annihilation, and destruction, Cummings is not without some glimmer of utopian hope in a better world: "In the course of the next ten thousand years it may be possible to find Delectable Mountains without going to prison—captivity I mean, *Monsieur Le Surveillant*—it may be possible, I dare say, to encounter Delectable Mountains who are not in prison" (p. 307). It may be that art itself will serve symbolically somehow to destroy habit and bring us to the Celestial City of the transcendent and living actuality, an art perhaps of satire and lyric.

iii

And what of Cummings' art in this book? He was twenty-eight when he wrote it and his style, in spite of its brilliance, is much more conventional than one realizes until it is compared with that of (say) *Eimi*, which was written eleven years later. It is a very skilful prose, and a very clear and serviceable prose, but it is also a very formal and somewhat pedantic prose. Except for scattered passages of impressionistic description, Cummings had not yet learned how to digest his intelligence, how to negate thinking by thinking. He had not yet learned, that is, how to make his instrument accord organically with his vision, his language recreate the actuality.

Take the opening of Chapter V, for example, which leads into his discussion of timelessness: "With the reader's permission I beg, at this point of my narrative, to indulge in one or two extrinsic observations" (p. 113). Although his use of this nineteenth-century authorial style is a bit ironic, and in certain satirical or comic parts is quite effective, the fact remains that it is his narrative instrument throughout, even when there is no need to be ironic. In his attack on The Great American Public as being too well educated—as opposed to his friends at La Ferté—to appreciate real art, as being too familiar with acceptable convention, that is, I think he tips his hand. For his style in this book is that of a very bright college boy, a very well-educated young man. And when he says "the diary or time method is a technique which cannot possibly do justice to timelessness," he may very well shift his manner of presentation, but he does not succeed in shifting his style. The strong simplicity of Bunyan, his model, did not influence him that far.

There are many exceptions, however, and these are usually impressionistic descriptions. Here he is speaking of eating in the prison dining room, for example: "The din was perfectly terrific. It had a minutely large quality. Here and there, in a kind of sonal darkness, solid sincere unintelligible absurd wisps of profanity heavily flickered. Etc." (p. 93). Passages like these are scattered like nuggets throughout, and they most closely resemble many of his early poems, being full of paradoxical and cumulative adjectival phrases, of strenuous verbs, of sharp images, and of abbreviated syntax. The point is, of course, that they stick out from the background of his more arid style a bit too conspicuously. In *Eimi* there is no such oil-and-water effect.

But it's not that *Eimi* is full of lyric poetry. An interesting demonstration of where these two books really touch one another stylistically is found in Chapter V. Cummings is concerned with describing a card game, and he gives two versions of it, one from his notebook and one which expands these notes: "In one of my numerous notebooks I have this perfectly direct paragraph:

> Card table: 4 stares play banque with 2 cigarettes (1 dead) & A pipe the clashing faces yanked by a leanness of one candle bottle-stuck (Birth of X) where sits The Clever Man who pyramids, sings (mornings) 'Meet Me . . .'

which specimen of telegraphic technique, being interpreted, means: Judas, Garibaldi, and The Holland Skipper (whom the reader will meet *de suite*)—Garibaldi's cigarette having gone out, so greatly is he absorbed—play *banque* with four intent and highly focused individuals who may or may not be The Schoolmaster, Monsieur Auguste, The Barber, and Même; with The Clever Man (as nearly always) acting as banker. Etc." (p. 133).

The thing is, of course, that the notebook version is closer to the actuality than the "interpretation." It may be harder for the reader to follow, and this is a problem I shall have to confront in discussing *Eimi*, but it is closer to the experience. What takes up less than five lines in the notes takes up three times as much space in the translation. This is because it is more direct, being limited as much as possible to what actually confronts the senses themselves, while the translation frames these sensata conceptually. And here we are again, back to the old problem of how to restore through language that which language deprives us of—direct contact with experience. This is probably what Blackmur meant, in "Notes on E. E. Cummings' Language" (1931), when he called Cummings a sensationalist, but what this austere critic missed, I think, is the transcendental metaphysic underlying

Cummings' obsession with directly contacting reality. What he wants is sensations not so much for their own sakes as for the sake of touching the living process of nature which creates them.

But Cummings had not yet discovered how to make better use of his "perfectly direct" notebooks, and so most of *The Enormous Room* is written in a style which interprets and translates experience instead of presenting it directly. Is that why it has been one of his most popular books—because it is relatively easy to read?

Tulips and Chimneys was first published in abridged form by Thomas Seltzer in 1923. The unabridged version, or archetype edition of the original manuscript, which dates from 1922, was not published until 1937, by the Golden Eagle Press. Comparison of these two versions reveals, however, that the omitted poems were in the meantime published in *&* (1925), *XLI Poems* (1925), and *is 5* (1926). The establishment of a proper chronology requires, therefore, a preliminary discussion of this rather tangled bibliographical problem.

The original manuscript contained 150 poems, including four which had been published in 1917 in *Eight Harvard Poets*. It is apparent that Seltzer reduced it to 66 poems, omitting 84. Although I don't think anyone knows exactly why he did it, I suspect that the manuscript was simply too large. And the principle he used may be inferred from the way he went about the job of winnowing the book down to size. He cut out poems from each of the original divisions, leaving some poems remaining in each, and thus preserving the over-all sequence and distribution of the original. He omitted 40 of the original 88 poems under the "TULIPS" heading, levying the heaviest toll on the "PORTRAITS" section (20 out of 30); and he omitted 44 of the original 64 poems under the "CHIMNEYS" heading, which represents a larger proportion of omissions in this part than in the first. It would appear, judging from the nature of the omitted poems, that

Seltzer wanted to deemphasize the stress which the original manuscript placed upon sex and the demimonde.

Cummings agreed in principle to this abridgement, but his feelings about other types of editing are expressed vividly in a letter to John Peale Bishop, who apparently was trying to help him place the manuscript and had found a taker:

Dear Bishop:

. . . Provided the arrangement isn't changed,I'm meek as to omissions—Not misprints or improvements,however happily conceived by however brilliant minds.

As for myself—

I don't give a [damn] . . .

whether the poems(as I have nicknamed the little objects) are published now hereafter or during the Interregnum Of Lenin: but if such luck befall them,it shall do so under my title, on this I am portland cement and carrara. Whether my title masturbates assininity,or no,has nothing to do with the subject. Also sprach Polyanna.

At any rate, Cummings had an opportunity two years later to print the 84 omitted poems: 43 went to *&*, which was privately printed and which contained 36 new poems in addition; and 41 went to *XLI Poems,* which was published by the Dial Press, and that of course is all this volume contains. Eight of the 43 which went to *&* appeared once again in the original version of *is 5,* while two of the new *&* poems were also reprinted there. *is 5* as we now have it in *Poems: 1923–1954* silently omits those 10 poems and returns them to *&*. The *Tulips and Chimneys* of this collected volume represents the 1923 Seltzer edition. The 1954 collection is, incidentally, misleadingly titled, for its earlier date is a year too late, while its later date gratuitously adds four years to its scope, since the last book included is *Xaipe* which appeared in 1950.

In my discussion of *Tulips and Chimneys,* I have reconstructed the original version and will regard its 150 poems as dating from 1922 or earlier, no matter when and where they finally appeared. *XLI Poems,* therefore, will simply not need separate treatment, since none of its pieces were new. Similarly, only the 36 new poems of *&* will need separate study. *is 5* will be analyzed as it now stands in the collected volume.

i

Tulips and Chimneys is Cummings' first and last volume of poetry which bears a conventional-looking title, which is strange, considering how strongly he insisted on retaining it here. One might think that "Tulips" referred to country poems and "Chimneys" to city poems, but this does not appear to be the case. I think it refers to a stylistic distinction, for most of the "Tulips" are in free verse, representing "natural" or "organic" structures, while all of the "Chimneys" are sonnets (sometimes tinkered with, but sonnets nevertheless), representing "fixed" or "artificial" structures. I will discuss these sections, and their accompanying subdivisions, in order.

There are three poems in the TULIPS section which have separate titles and do not belong to any of the subdivisions: "Epithalamion," a long erotic celebration of the coming of spring; "Of Nicolette," a dreamy evocation of a lady in a moonlit medieval scene; and "Puella Mea," a lengthy celebration of the speaker's lady and her physical charms. I would guess that these are very early poems, predating even the 1917 poems, for they are very literary and derivative indeed, reminding one especially of Shelley, Keats, Swinburne, and Rossetti (a4):

> And still the mad magnificent herald Spring
> assembles beauty from forgetfulness
> with the wild trump of April. . . .

But there is still a distinctive Cummingsesque flair for language here (a3):

> Thou aged unreluctant earth who dost
> with quivering continual thighs invite
> the thrilling rain the slender paramour
> to toy with thy extraordinary lust. . . .

These poems are not, of course, in free verse, and represent an exception to the rule I believe underlies the TULIPS classification. "Epithalamion" contains twenty-one eight-line pentameter stanzas, "Of Nicolette" contains four eight-line pentameter stanzas, and "Puella Mea" contains seven-and-a-half pages of irregularly rhyming tetrameter lines.

The bulk of the TULIPS section is divided into eight labeled groups. It is unnecessary to find a strict rationale to explain these subdivisions, for some of the poems which Seltzer rejected changed groups when they were finally published in 1925. In *XLI Poems,* for example, the group labeled SONGS contains poems which originally came from SONGS, IMPRESSIONS, PORTRAITS, and AMORES. Similarly, the group labeled SONNETS lumps together poems which had originally been divided into SONNETS-REALITIES, SONNETS-UNREALITIES, and SONNETS-ACTUALITIES. But there are, nevertheless, some significant distinguishing traits:

SONGS originally contained ten poems (four were omitted). These are mostly about love, dreams, and death. Cummings' style is still rather derivative here, for there are Ninetyish and Twentyish touches, with glimmers of the Caveliers, Herrick, and Victorian medievalism. The approach is not very experimental, and only one is in free verse.

CHANSON INNOCENTES originally contained five poems (two were omitted). They are all about children, and experimentation appears to begin here. There are free verse poems, lines are spaced unconventionally and the free verse visual stanza—a typographical construction in which lines are grouped according to some pattern other than those provided by rhyme and meter—is used. I would guess that Cummings had Blake in mind when he used this heading, and I think there are significant parallels between that poet's Innocence-Experience dichotomy and Cummings' lyric-satire, rural-urban, and realities-unrealities dichotomies. I am not sure, however, why this particular heading is in French.

ORIENTALE originally contained six poems (none were rejected). These contain an erotic-exotic treatment of lust. Again I am not sure why the title is in French, unless Cummings had Flaubert in mind. These poems are somewhat experimental, and VI even foreshadows the future use of typographical devices.

AMORES originally contained eleven poems (three were omitted). All except two deal, of course, with love, and these two deal with fall. By now the language seems to be growing more original (a37, no. VII):

> *O Distinct*
> *Lady of my unkempt adoration*
> *if i have made*
> *a fragile certain*
>
> *song under the window of your soul. . . .*

Many of these poems are free of the literary echoes and fashions which clogged the preceding poems. The effect and placing of "Distinct," "unkempt," and "fragile certain," for example, create a characteristic Cummingsesque tone and rhythm.

LA GUERRE originally contained five poems (three were rejected). Three deal with the First World War directly, while two are satirical treatments of man's intellect and his materialism. Apparently "La Guerre" refers to the individual's battle with society as well as to the War itself! A hint of experimental punctuation appears in "O sweet spontaneous" (a39–40, no. II), and the language seems to be emerging as Cummings' early adjectival style, a style which was fashioned to startle, to shock by paradox, surprise, juxtaposition, and the unusual. Freshness is all (a39, no. I):

> *i say that sometimes*
> *on these long talkative animals*
> *are laid fists of huger silence. . . .*

IMPRESSIONS originally contained nine poems (four were omitted).

PORTRAITS originally contained thirty poems (twenty were omitted).

POST IMPRESSIONS originally contained ten poems (four were omitted). These three groups are best considered together, for I do not find any perceptible principle of division here. The labels clearly imply a descriptive poetry, and what one finds here is the evolution of a sensibility responding imaginatively to the physical world: places, times of day, seasons, dreams, people, the demimonde, time, and death (a47, no. IV):

> *i walked the boulevard*
>
> *i saw a dirty child*
> *skating on noisy wheels of joy.*

Typographical devices are increasingly in evidence, called into being by the necessities of the subject-matter (a84, no. XIV):

inthe,exquisite;

morning   sure   lyHer eye s exactly sit,ata little round-table . . .

And the style is becoming increasingly violent and experimental (a78, no. VIII):

> *. . . the slobbering walls filthily*
> *push witless creases of screaming warmth . . .*

There are three labelled groups in the CHIMNEYS section.

SONNETS-REALITIES originally contained twenty-one poems (fifteen were omitted). These deal primarily with sexual love and the demimonde, and the style is correspondingly mixed and violent.

SONNETS-UNREALITIES originally contained seventeen poems (eleven were omitted). This section deals mainly with idealized romantic love, as the title would seem to imply, and with the world of nature's seasons, the night, the sea, death, and time. The style here is generally less experimental than in the other two sonnet groups.

SONNETS-ACTUALITIES   originally   contained twenty-three poems (eighteen were omitted). The poems here combine a treatment of ideal and sexual love, the seasons, places, times of day, dream, and death. Their style is tender, paradoxical, whimsical, and more experimental than in the other two groups.

Perhaps a word is in order here about Cummings' use of the sonnet. The first point of significance is their quantity: there are 61 sonnets in *Tulips and Chimneys* out of 150 poems, which represents a proportion of about 40 per cent. The proportion of sonnets in *&* is even higher — 18 out of 36, or just one-half. Although the proportion drops in the succeeding volumes — generally to about a fourth — the number remains significant. The total is 191 out of 707, or between a quarter and a third. The second point is their subject matter. Carrying the tradition of poetic love one step further, Cummings deals with sex, prostitutes, and the demimonde, finding thereby a place in these little rooms of rhyme for the worlds of reality and actuality as well as for that of unreality. And the third point is their style, for he bends these fourteen-line structures to the breaking point, spacing them unconventionally, twisting the meter, employing typographical devices, using rough diction, and so on. If William Carlos Williams has scorned the sonnet, reserving his praise only for the rather casual products of Merrill Moore's filing cabinets, Cummings has tried to make of it a moment's monument indeed.

In the second of his *six nonlectures* (pp. 28–30), Cummings discusses the three poetic periods he went through as a boy. His first produced childish poems "combining fearless expression with keen observation," but his second saw him caught up in a passion for messages and social justice. It was not until his third period that his "eager energies" were diverted "from what to how: from substance to structure." He became fascinated by the fact "that there are all kinds of intriguing verse-forms, chiefly French; and that each of these forms can and does exist in and of itself, apart from the use to which you or I may not or may put it." One day during this third period he met Josiah Royce in the street, who asked him whether he was acquainted with the sonnets of Dante Gabriel Rossetti. Upon receiving a negative answer, the sage invited the young poet into his study and read Rossetti to him. "And very possibly (although I don't, as usual, know) that is the reason—or more likely the unreason—I've been writing sonnets ever since."

I want to stress, then, Cummings' traditionalism and his respect for poetic forms. If he distorts what he receives into experimental shapes, the fact that he is working within a convention should not be overlooked. Nor should the fact that he is rooted in the past be recognized with the raised eyebrows of surprise (see Alfred Kazin's review of *six nonlectures, New Yorker,* January 2, 1954, pp. 57–59). The poets whose poems he recited at the end of each nonlecture—Wordsworth, Chaucer, Shakespeare, Swinburne, Donne, Dante, Keats, Shelley, and so on—are indeed from some sort of Golden Treasury. But when was that ever a bar to any watch we keep? These are not exactly Bryant, Longfellow, Whittier, and James Russell Lowell! Cummings need not be pegged as an Anarchist to be appreciated, neither does this mean he is just another Ella Wheeler Wilcox in modernist disguise. Let us beware of false disjunctions.

But what is the significance of *Tulips and Chimneys* as a whole in relation to Cummings' development? Most of his characteristic subjects are here, even at the beginning: spring, love, twilight, the city, the country, sex, the demimonde, dream, time, death, children, war, society, and so on. But it is a world—and this time Blackmur is right—of a sensationalist, a world to confront and ingest, a matrix with which some day to come to terms, a world almost without thought (a148, no. VII*) :

> my mind is
> a big hunk of irrevocable nothing which touch and
> taste and smell and hearing and sight keep hitting and
> chipping with sharp fatal tools
> in an agony of sensual chisels i perform squirms of
> chrome and execute strides of cobalt
> nevertheless i
> feel that i cleverly am being altered that i slightly am
> becoming something a little different, in fact
> myself
> Hereupon helpless i utter lilac shrieks and scarlet
> bellowings.

There are, it is true, several hints of things to come, of ideas, evaluations, and concepts anticipating those of the mature poet. See, for example, "O sweet spontaneous" (a39–40, no. II), "Humanity i love you" (a151–152, no. II), "the hours rise up" (a42–43, no. IV), and a few others which similarly oppose thought and feeling, society and the individual. But I fail to find here any specific expression of the central notion of the timeless and transcendent world, in spite of the fact, as I have noted before, that there are such expressions in the Lachaise essay and *The Enormous Room*, both of which were published before *Tulips and Chimneys*. This is the course, then, which I see Cummings' development as taking: from a raw confrontation of the squirming world to a growing awareness of its meaning and significance; and technically, from a violent and amorphous style to a discovery of a unique and personal instrument to embody that growing awareness.

For if this volume represents a discovery of the world, it also represents the discovery of language; as he makes the effort to grasp the bulging universe, he tries at the same time to come to grips with the pleasures and torments of words. Language is like a new toy in his hands, and he cannot twirl and swing it too much; he goes to extremes to see what it can do; he bends and twists it to see if it will break; he bangs and kicks it to find it it's hollow. But all the time you feel he loves it, is delighted and amazed by it, and cannot keep his hands away from it. He is wild,

calm, reverent, whimsical, paradoxical, serious and witty
by turns; he uses rough diction and formal diction; he
writes free verse poems, prose poems, and sonnets; and he
develops early his use of the free verse visual stanza and
certain typographical devices.

But, with one or two exceptions, he has not yet developed his satirical mode, his conceptual vocabulary, or
his use of syntactical displacement. Though much has
been done, much yet remains to be done. He is
cleverly being altered and is slightly becoming something a little different.

ii

Since the developments three years later in *&* are
not particularly striking, we need not linger long here.
There are 79 poems in this volume: 43 came from the
original *Tulips and Chimneys* manuscript, and 36 appear to be new. It is with these latter that we shall primarily be concerned.

The book is divided into three parts, labelled "A,"
"N," and "D." The first seems to correspond to the
TULIPS section of *Tulips and Chimneys*, containing
POST IMPRESSIONS and PORTRAITS; while the
third appears to correspond to the CHIMNEYS section,
containing SONNETS-REALITIES and SONNETS-
ACTUALITIES. The middle or "N" section is labelled
"&: SEVEN POEMS" and consists entirely of new
poems. One would think, then, that the title of the book
means two related things: that it contains poems left over
from the 1922 manuscript, and new poems added for the
present purpose.

A) POST IMPRESSIONS contains thirteen poems
(eight new). These deal with the city, times of day,
weather, life, sex, and death. PORTRAITS contains
twelve poems (three are new). The subjects here are a
whorehouse, woman, and little Effie.

N) Contains seven poems (all are new). The usual
subjects are in evidence, along with an increase in stylistic and technical experimentation

D) SONNETS-REALITIES   contains   twenty-two

poems (nine are new). These are primarily about the demimonde, and are quite experimental. SONNETS-ACTUALITIES contains twenty-four poems (nine are new). The sonnets in this group are generally concerned with sex, love, death, the seasons, street scenes, and times of day. They are relatively less experimental.

The significance of this book for Cummings' development seems to me to be found mainly in one innocent-appearing little poem, beginning "who knows if the moon's" (a103, no. VII). As the slight touches of transcendentalism and of the satirical vision were the exceptions which proved the rule in *Tulips and Chimneys,* so too are they here. But this poem seems to present an image which, in the light of the mature work, could very well be a symbol of the transcendental world. The poet imagines here that the moon is a balloon which will carry us higher "than houses and steeples and clouds" into "a keen city which nobody's ever visited,where"

> *always*
> *it's*
> *Spring)and everyone's*
> *in love and flowers pick themselves*

This city, of course, is the world of the transcendental vision, the world of perpetual rebirth, of surrender, and of harmony with nature.

iii

is 5 comes equipped with a "Foreword," which explains the title, and five numbered divisions in accordance with that title. Counting the first "I FIVE AMERICANS" as one poem, the original 1926 edition of this volume contained eighty-four poems. But since ten had already appeared in *&* (eight of which had come in turn from the 1922 *Tulips and Chimneys* manuscript), these have been returned there in the complete collection of 1954. There are thus seventy-four poems in *is 5* as we now have it.

Although the five numbered divisions are not further

labelled or broken by the poet into sub-groups, I think they may be analyzed and divided as follows. ONE Contains thirty-four poems, and these are mostly in free verse except for the first group of five sonnets. This section may be subdivided into three groups—Satires, Comedies, and Other Observations.

Satires—contains thirteen poems. These attack our pieties, categories, and institutions (II, IV, V, VII, VIII, XI, XIV, XV, XVI, XVII, XXI, XXV, XXVII). The targets are the mass mind, romantic nostalgia, a college graduate, Freudianism, a priest, an unlovely couple in a restaurant, big shots, the old people who run the world, American tourists, and so on. Although his ridicule is somewhat lacking in discrimination, depending too readily upon a certain vagueness in focusing on the enemy (who *is* that "deadfromtheneckup graduate," anyway?), Cummings' values are beginning to be more clearly defined. Here, too, the style is appropriately experimental, for we should be beginning to sense that there is an organic relation between the poet's techniques and his purposes. It will soon appear that in general Cummings uses metrical stanzas for his more "serious" poems, and reserves his experiments by and large for his free verse embodiments of satire, comedy, and description. Parody, pun, slang, and typographical distortion are called into being by the urgencies of the satirical mode, which requires the dramatic rendition of scorn, wit, and ridicule. Violence in the meaning: violence in the style. Similarly, as we shall see, the movement required of a descriptive poem calls in turn for somewhat similar distortions. Motion in the mind: motion in the eye.

Comedies—contains eight poems. There is motion, exuberance, and flamboyance here as in the satires, but here the intention is not so much scorn as it is fun. These are jokes, tours de force of gaiety and laughter (III, VI, X, XVIII, XIX, XX, XXIV, XXXII). These are the poems about Professor Royce forgetting his tie, Jimmie's goil, Uncle Sol, mr youse, that new "car," Amy Lowell, and so on. It has often been remarked that the transcendental vision is not commonly accompanied by a sense of humor. One does not easily picture Blake, Coleridge, Carlyle, Emerson, or Thoreau as laughing. But perhaps it is a distinguishing mark in Cummings that his conception of joy is somewhat less severe, and that his love of woman and of nature is not simply strenuously dutiful. This surrealistic euphoria, in combination with such a clear vision of society's ills and of the seamier sides of life, is indeed rare in English and American literature in general. Who else, except for Henry Miller, can laugh with such exhilaration? The sexual joy in Lawrence is grim by comparison.

Other Observations—contains thirteen poems. Here I have placed his five prostitutes, his man oppressed by marriage, his poem about Tom Larson, his picture of old ladies in the sun, and so on (I, IX, XII, XIII, XXII, XXIII, XXVI, XXVIII, XXIX, XXX, XXXI, XXXIII, XXXIV).

TWO Contains ten poems, primarily about the War, and mostly in free verse. Several of these are satires and comedies, and several are more in the nature of laments and elegies. THREE Contains seven poems, all of which appear to be European vignettes and landscapes.

FOUR Contains eighteen poems, most of which concern the lover and his lady. FIVE Contains five poems, all of which are love sonnets.

Now the primary thing about *is 5* is, of course, the advance made in Cummings' satirical vision. With only a few exceptions ("the Cambridge ladies," a58, no I; "here is little Effie's head," a95, X; "Humanity i love you," a151, no. II), the preceding two volumes were almost devoid of satire. But it starts here and remains generally constant in the later volumes, occupying anywhere from a fifth to a third of each book. It does not spring fully-formed from the brow of Zeus, however, for by my count Cummings published thirteen satirical prose essays (*Miscellany*, pp. 109–83) between the end of 1924 and the beginning of 1926 (& was published in February of 1925, and *is 5* in June of 1926). These are concerned with various follies in the arts (movies, magazines, playhouses, art, poetry, etc.), the world of society (success in business, etc.), and politics (Coolidge and the Dawes Plan). On these issues and in this way did he sharpen his teeth in preparation for *is 5*. It is as if he were learning negatively, by contrast, to define his values.

Not that there is no positive definition as well, although we have a wait of five years before his vision begins to emerge explicitly and authoritatively in his poems. Look, for example, at the poem beginning "voices to voices" (a189-90, no. XXXIII), in which he is beginning to sense the use of such constructions as "undying" to mean "merely existing." Or at the well known "since feeling is first" (a208-9, no. VII), in which the love-compliment is transcendental rather than merely erotic or romantic. Love, indeed, appears in over forty poems in this volume, overbalancing the satires twice over, and is conceived of in terms which are more gentle than those of the witty and paradoxical lover of *Tulips and Chimneys* and *&*. Correspondingly, the emphasis on sex and the demimonde seems to be diminishing.

The "Foreword" to *is 5* (a163), which his publishers asked him to write, also requires comment, for Cummings' transcendentalism is more explicit here than anywhere else in the volume. Here he makes three related points: (1) that his techniques aim at "that precision which creates movement," (2) that he has this aim because he is more concerned with process than product, and (3) that this concern is rooted in a transcendental conception of truth as an unmeasurable mystery (2 times 2 is 5) in opposition to the empirical conception of truth as fact (2 times 2 is 4). The "logic" of this might be seen as truth = process = movement—that is, the living dynamic reality. Hence, his techniques are to be understood in relation to his attempt to embody this truth in the service of this "obsession" with "Making." Experimental technique is the means whereby the poet tries to reproduce in the reader's mind the vital flux of becoming which he (the poet) sees in life. The odd thing is that his experiments seem to me to be less flamboyant here than they were in the preceding two books, although he is developing a greater sense of the possibilities of the visual stanza, having learned by now that it can be built cumulatively as well as symmetrically.

And of the utmost significance, finally, is the disappearance of any trace of "literary" influence. For it is one thing to work within the traditions of the great poets, and quite another to try to sound like them. Fresh, original, exuberant, experimental yet traditional, *is 5* is Cummings' first consistently characteristic book of poems.

Him is a play which is so fluid, dynamic, heterogeneous, vital, and alive that it is difficult to find a way to its center. It presents a varied and complex surface to the beholder, and he looks almost in vain for a handhold. Cummings speaks, in the *Imaginary Dialogue Between an Author and a Public* which was printed on the inside flap of the original edition's jacket, of people who have discovered "the third voice of 'life,' which believes itself and which cannot mean because it is." He says, "They are good for nothing except walking upright in the cordial revelation of the fatal reflexive." This third voice is discovered "in a mirror surrounded with mirrors." The Public then asks: "And your play is all about one of these persons, Mr. Author?" And Cummings replies: "Perhaps. But (let me tell you a secret) I rather hope my play is one of these persons" (Norman, pp. 225–26).

i

In order to clarify his intentions here, let us resume what we already know of Cummings' theory of art, and then see how it applies to the writing of this play—which was meant, after all, for the stage. Art, for him, imitates nature; since nature is organic, art must also be organic; therefore, a work of art, in capturing the process of becoming, will *become* something itself, a Verb, an Is. It is not *about* something, it *is* something; it doesn't mean anything, it exists. And for the artist, success in art means self-discovery, self-knowledge, and being himself, for only in that way will he get in firsthand touch with the living reality within as well as the living reality without. That is what is meant, I think, by "the cordial revelation of the fatal reflexive."

If this is the third voice of life, what are the other two "voices"? Cummings tells his Public: "And so far as you're concerned 'Life' is a verb of two voices—active, to do, and passive, to dream. Others believe doing to be only a kind of dreaming. Still others have discovered (in a mirror surrounded with mirrors), something harder than silence but softer than falling; the third voice of 'life,' which believes itself and which cannot mean because it is." The two voices represent the ordinary view of life, which separates doing and dreaming, believing in the former and distrusting the latter. It is the view which says, as Cummings' Public says, "So far as I'm concerned, my very dear sir, nonsense isn't everything in life." I don't know who the first "Others" represent, but it seems to me that they see life in terms of synthesis rather than antithesis, although they do not have the full artistic vision. For "Still Others" are artists for whom dreaming is doing.

And surely, as we shall see, the play deals with self-discovery, mirrors, and dreams. Thus, Cummings wrote on the program when the play was first produced at the Provincetown Playhouse in the spring of 1928: "WARNING: *him* isn't a comedy or a tragedy or a farce or a melodrama or a revue or an operetta or a moving picture or any other convenient excuse 'for going to the theatre'—in fact, it's a PLAY, so let it PLAY; and because you are here, let it PLAY with you. . . . Don't try to despise it, let it try to despise you. Don't try to enjoy it, let it try to enjoy you. DON'T TRY TO UNDERSTAND IT, LET IT TRY TO UNDERSTAND YOU" (Norman, pp. 238–39).

How, then, does this theory of art apply to Cummings' conception of the theatre? Much help is found in a group of his essays, written just before this play appeared. In "The Adult, the Artist and the Circus" (1925), he describes the circus "as a gigantic spectacle; *which is sur-rounded by an* audience,—in contrast to our modern theatres, where an audience and a spectacle merely confront each other—Movement is the very stuff out of which this dream is made. Or we may say that movement is the content, the subject-matter, of the circus-show, while bigness is its form; provided we realise that here (as in all true 'works of art') content and form are aspects of a homageneous whole" (*Miscellany*, p. 47).

In "Coney Island" (1926), he sees the amusement park as "a perfectly unprecedented fusion of the circus and the theatre. It resembles the theatre, in that it fosters every known species of illusion. It suggests the circus, in that it puts us in touch with whatever is hair-raising, breath-taking and pore-opening. But Coney has a distinct drop on both theatre and circus. Whereas at the theatre we merely are deceived, at Coney we deceive ourselves. Whereas at the circus we are merely spectators of the impossible, at Coney we ourselves perform impossible feats." As he stressed the homogeneity (organic form) of the circus, so he says here about Coney Island, that "the essence of Coney Island's 'circus-theatre' consists in *homogeneity*. THE AUDIENCE IS THE PERFORMANCE, and vice versa." Then he concludes by saying, "Two facts are gradually becoming recognized: first, that the circus is an authentic 'theatric' phenomenon and second, that the conventional 'theatre' is a box of negligible tricks" (*Miscellany*, pp. 55–56).

The picture-frame stage is thus inorganic, mechanical, and sterile, for it persists in thrusting conventional illusion-making devices between performance and audience—it separates "to act" and "to dream." In "The Theatre: I" (1926), Cummings castigates what he calls the "pennyintheslot peepshow parlour" (*Miscellany*, p. 73), and in "The Theatre: II" (1926), he spells out, with the help of Friedrich Kiesler, the alternative. The peep-show stage substitutes static surface for dynamic space, thus scene (surface) and actor (space) negate each other and no organic cohesion is possible. In the "space-stage," on

54   E. E. CUMMINGS

the other hand, the stage is empty, functioning as space; it has ceased to appeal as decoration. The play itself is required to give it life; everything now depends on the play, which is not separated from the audience. Thus is created an organic relation between actors and stage, play and theatre, performance and audience (*Miscellany*, pp. 75–77).

ii

I think it can be safely assumed that Cummings had these ideals in mind when he wrote *Him*. He uses a room with a window and a mirror for the Him-Me scenes, but he rotates it four times during the course of the play, so that it ends where it began, with actors and audience confronting one another through the invisible mirror. One of the things which is accomplished by this device—and it is not the only one—is that the audience is encouraged to regard the room as having four walls, and not as having three walls plus an illusory fourth. Another thing it accomplishes is to make symbolic play with the window and the mirror. But most of the other scenes—the surrealistic ones—are played in space rather than in a picture-frame. In this way depth and movement are created.

But there is much more to the organicity of this play than mere staging. Written into the action are certain much more crucial devices, devices which are literary as much as they are theatrical. In the first place, the central situation—the conflict between Me and Him, and its resolution—is presented only by indirection. Indeed, this is one of the main reasons why the play is so difficult to interpret. With a skill surpassing that of Hemingway in "Hills Like White Elephants," Cummings builds the dialogue between his two distraught lovers so that the audience only gradually discovers—that is, "naturally" or organically—that the girl's pregnancy is threatening to cause their separation. Not only the dialogue, however, but the recurrence of repeated birth-references serves to convey implicitly what is happening. Then there is, of course, the framing device of the placard picturing a doctor anesthetizing a woman, and the climactic emergence of Me with a baby at the freak show.

"This play of mine is all about mirrors," says Him toward the end of Act I (p. 29). And speaking of framing devices, this play of Cummings is full of mirror-like repetitions and symmetries. The Doctor, the one who is anesthetizing Me on the placard which serves as the backdrop for the Misses Weird scenes, keeps reappearing in different disguises throughout. He is called "a harmless magician," "a master of illusion," and "his name is Nascitur" (p. 132). The structure of Act I is balanced: two Him-Me scenes framed by three scenes involving the Misses Weird. And Act III is similarly, although more complexly, balanced. On the placard furthermore, as the head of the woman is being anesthetized, Me's eyes close at the beginning of Act I, and they open in the middle of the last act. And, of course, her baby is born at end. The second act consists of scenes from the play written by the hero of Him's play, the Man in the Mirror, who is writing a play about a man writing a play. The Gentleman (played by the Doctor) is just about to be reborn at the end of Act II, thereby paralleling the birth of Me's baby at the end of Act III. Both Him and Me are aware of other selves which each has created for the other. All the characters of Act II reappear at the end of Act III, thereby creating an intersection between the world of Him and Me and that of the Man in the Mirror's play. And at the end, another such intersection occurs between actors and audience.

When taken by themselves, of course, these echoes are just devices, mechanisms. When seen in the light of Cummings' theory of art and his conception of the theatre, however, they take on added significance as means for achieving that organicity, the fatal reflexivity, he believes is necessary to a real work of art. The result is a globed, rounded thing, almost impenetrable from the outside. But if this is so, then their final significance (if one can say anything is final in such matters) must be found in the way they function in the whole. One does not merely want to put actors and audience into living contact with one another; one does not merely try to write a play consisting of reflecting devices. One does these things because one has an action to present to the audience, an experience to dramatize, a plot to convey, a story to tell.

iii

What is the story of *Him*—its plot—and what does it add up to? This is the real difficulty of the play, for it is in itself enjoyable to read and exciting to see on the stage. It *is* intensely alive, as Cummings says all good art should be. And what he says of burlesque applies here as well: "the fact that this highly stylised, inherently 'abstract,' positively 'futuristic' art known to its devotees as burlesk is indubitably *for the masses*, knocks into a cocked chapeau the complaint of many so-called 'critics' that 'modern art' is 'neurotic,' 'unhealthy,' 'insane,' 'arbitrary,' 'unessential,' 'superficial' and 'not for the masses' " ("You Aren't Mad, Am I?" 1925, *Miscellany*, p. 69). When read or seen uncritically, it is as much fun as a circus. Are we then not to read it critically, taking the author's advice not to try to understand it? I think it all depends on how we go about it: something is there calling for interpretation, but we'll never find it if we persist in trying to make the play fit categories which don't apply. That's what I think Cummings' WARNING is all about. If a good work is organic in being itself, then a good critic should be organic too, in reading it in terms of its own purposes. And he needn't miss the fun of the play in the process of interpreting it.

Robert Maurer provides a good basis for further work (*Bucknell Review*, VI [May 1956], 1–27). He sees the heart of the play as residing in the four Me-Him scenes, and he interprets these as comprising a tragedy of crosspurposes. At the beginning, Him is caught in a conflict between his art and his beloved, and senses that she loves only a part of him. Similarly, Me, who is pregnant, is afraid he loves her for the wrong reasons—that she is intelligent and is interested in cleverness and ideas. The irony is that he loves her for what she is—beautiful, alive, intuitive. He doesn't know that she's pregnant and can't understand why she's fretting; nor is he sure about himself and his art. She decides to end the affair, however, because she wants to free him for his art, and this just at the time when he's beginning to see the possibility of reconciling the two. I have not done justice to the fullness and perceptiveness of Mr. Maurer's analysis, but these are the main points. I want to go on from here to Cummings' own interpretations.

Maurer rightly points out that Cummings later saw, in *six nonlectures* (1953), that art was not the only way to self-transcendence, and that it was the lack of this insight which troubled him and his play in 1927. A passage from the Introduction to the Modern Library edition (1932) of *The Enormous Room* underscores this dichotomy:

> Thanks to I dare say my art I am able to become myself.
> Well well! [replies the Public] Doesn't that sound as if people who weren't artists couldn't become themselves?
> Does it?
> What do you think happens to people who aren't artists? What do you think people who aren't artists become?
> I feel they don't become: I feel nothing happens to them; I feel negation becomes of them (pp. ix–x).

But in the fifth nonlecture, twenty-one years later, Cummings can say: "We should go hugely astray in assuming that art was the only selftranscendence. Art is a mystery; all mysteries have their source in a mystery-of-mysteries who is love: and if lovers may reach eternity directly through love herself, their mystery remains essentially that of the loving artist whose way must lie through his art, and of the loving worshipper whose aim is oneness with his god. From another point of view, every human being is in and of himself or herself illimitable; but the essence of his or her illimitability is precisely its uniqueness—nor could all poetry (past present and future) begin to indicate the varieties of selfhood; and conse-

quently of selftranscendence" (p. 82). In talking specifically of *Him*, however, he does not emphasize the conflict between his protagonist and his heroine over this issue. On the other hand, he does provide a clue when he
says the play revolves "the distinction between time and
eternity, measurable when and illimitable now" (p. 79).

Let us keep these distinctions in mind, for they tie in
well with a passage from a letter which Cummings wrote
(November 8, 1961) in answer to my questions about
the play: "any 'conflict' between Him & Me is to my
feeling,based on the fortunate difference between art &
life;man & woman;the ultimate reality of an individual's
imagination,& whatever mostpeople agree to call 'real.' "
Then he fortunately gets more specific, going beyond his
discussion in *six nonlectures*: "Him's deepest wish is to
compose a miraculously intense play-of-art—Me's underlying ambition is to be entirely loved by someone through
whom she may safely have a child. He loves,not herself,but
the loveliness of his mistress;she loves,not himself,but
the possibility of making a husband out of a lover. For
him,sexual ecstasy is a form of selftranscendence:for
her,it's a means to an end(motherhood)." Of Me, he
says, "She has 'no mind'; but possesses something minutely
more powerful than either intellect or intelligence:the
Intuition whose triumph constitutes the play's final
scene." This refers, of course, to her insight into the fact
that the fourth or mirror-wall facing the audience is invisible, and that those real people out there are pretending
the room and the lovers are real:

> HIM (*standing in the middle of the room, whispers*):
> I wish I could believe this.
> ME (*Smiles, shaking her head*): You can't.
> HIM (*Staring at the invisible wall*): Why?
> ME: Because this is true.

CURTAIN

What, then, is the play about—or rather, what *is* the
play? I'm not sure about certain things even now. Maurer
says, as have others, that the whole play is Me's dream

while under anesthesia. But this doesn't entirely work for me. And why is Me, if she possesses something more powerful than intellect or intelligence, so opposed in her desire for motherhood to Him, the artist? For the artist too is supposed to have this triumphant Intuition. Perhaps because Him is only partially an artist so far. Why, if Him loves this intuitiveness in her, does he not understand her? Is it because she's divided in herself—between her desire to be clever for him and her need to be herself? What, then, has motherhood to do with it? If Him loves Me not for what she is but as a beautiful mistress, what then *is* she? A woman who wants a husband and a baby? If Me loves him not for what he is but as a husband and father, what then is *he?* An artist? But if they loved each other for what they really are, what would it be? An artist loving a mother; a mother loving an artist? And if Cummings can speak of "the fortunate difference between art and life," what then becomes of Maurer's point about trying to reconcile them and of the passage quoted from *six nonlectures?*

Perhaps Shaw's preface to *Man and Superman* will help us out here. Women, says Shaw, intuitively fulfill Nature's procreative purpose by entrapping men in the sexual web. Only men of genius are exempt from these lures, for they have an equally strong drive, "men selected by Nature to carry on the work of building up an intellectual consciousness of her own instinctive purpose." He continues: "Accordingly, we observe in the man of genius all the unscrupulousness and all the 'self-sacrifice' (the two things are the same) of Woman. He will risk the stake and the cross; starve, when necessary, in a garret all his life; study women and live on their work and care as Darwin studied worms and lived upon sheep; work his nerves to rags without payment, a sublime altruist in his disregard of himself, an atrocious egotist in his disregard of others. Here Woman meets a purpose as impersonal, as irresistible as her own; and the clash is sometimes tragic" (Penguin ed., pp. xx–xxi).

For Cummings, however, this is only part of the story.

The tragedy in this play, as Mauer believes, is that its hero is caught in a moment of transition from being Shaw's Artist to becoming Cummings' Lover, for he is committed to his lady as well as to his work. Or perhaps it would be more accurate to say that he is caught between being a divided man—a would-be artist plus a domesticated husband—and becoming a whole man—and therefore an actual artist because he can love. That is why there are so many mirror-like "identities" in the play: he is not sure who he is, and the point is that he doesn't ever really find out during the course of the play. The mature Cummings would say that being an artist depends upon being able to love, and that loving depends upon knowing and hence transcending oneself. In *six nonlectures* he interprets the "Damn everything but the circus" passage in terms of "three mysteries: love, art, and selftranscendence or growing" (p. 81). The last two of this triad had been worked out as early as April, 1927 (the same year *Him* appeared), in an essay called "The Agony of the Artist (with a Capital A)": "It is Art because it is *alive*. . . . we have made a profound error in trying to *learn* Art, since whatever Art stands for is whatever *cannot* be learned. Indeed, the Artist is no other than he who unlearns what he has learned, in order to know *himself*; and the agony of the Artist, far from being the result of the world's failure to discover and appreciate him, arises from his own personal struggle to discover, to appreciate and finally to express himself. . . . 'to become an Artist' means nothing: whereas to become alive, or one's self, means everything" (*Miscellany*, pp. 89–90).

But the first term of this triad does not achieve clear expression until 1953, in *six nonlectures*: "Art is a mystery; all mysteries have their source in a mystery-of-mysteries who is love . . ." (p. 82). There is, of course, all the poetry which was to be written during this 26-year span, but as we have already noted, Cummings' notion of the central role of love in the transcendent vision had not yet appeared in the poetry preceding this play. And it is no wonder, for as the mystery-of-mysteries, love involves a paradox which it takes most people years to learn, some people never: self-discovery can become self-transcendence (Cummings uses the terms interchangeably in the *non-lectures* passage) only through love, which means giving, surrender. To be oneself, in other words, is to be strong and true enough to give oneself to another freely and without rewards or conditions; it is only the person who is afraid to be himself that takes when in love, for he needs the reassurance of another's devotion to give him what he cannot have by himself. Thus does self-knowledge lead to love, and love to art.

The "plot" of *Him*, then, concerns a "would-be artist" (the phrase is Cummings') who is coming to realize the nature of his problem, who is beginning to discover, in other words, that he is unable to write his play because he is unable to love. And he is unable to love because he doesn't know who he is and is therefore unsure of himself. He is coming to realize the nature of his problem, as I say, but he does not come to solve it. Realization is resolution when formally considered, however, although it is a tentative and ambiguous way to end a play. But, faithful to his organic ideal, Cummings is trying to be true and natural, and to avoid the pasted-on ending. As his hero says, in his bitter mirror-soliloquy after having another misunderstanding with his lady: "Where's the moment—come: for an incipient dramatist you're an unearthly blockhead. You maul the climaxes always. . . . The well-known writer of scenarios, properties one million lemon pies, hero a spitball artist of the first water, much furniture everywhere broken, pity and terror incorporated, it all comes out in the wash, happy ending, I've got the machine who's got the god?" (p. 22). She had asked him to write things the public would like, and he had replied: "Aha! I see it all now: The Great American Novel (gimme a chord, professor)—Lucy T. Wot felt That Something which is nothing like anything, and as quick as everything laying her red hot pail of blackberries down in the midafternoon moonlight, slowly raised two eyes, in both after each of which a single tear strove as it were for the mastery, to those of Henery Pudd who merely looked at her however" (p. 20).

Nevertheless, it may be of help to infer what a solution would be in order that we may come to a clearer view of the nature of the problem, for if we can see what would be right we will be better able to see what is wrong. Cummings speaks, in his letter, of "the fortunate *difference* between art & life; etc.," and yet his hero cries out toward the end of the play, "How should what is desirable shut us entirely from what is?" (p. 130). The answer to this apparent dilemma is implied in this passage from *six nonlectures*: "On the one hand a complete fanatic, dedicated to values beyond life and death, [Him] is on the other hand a profoundly alive and supremely human being" (p. 81). Cummings has been analyzing the loneliness of the artist, and has paused to stress the paradox that this artist also is "deeply identified" with his lady. The resolution toward which Him is groping, then, and which he cannot quite reach, involves coming to grips with paradox: to dream is to do, to surrender is to win. Just as the spiritual ideal, in the "Foreword to Krazy," is different from, yet needs, the real, so too does art need life, and so too does man need woman.

The resolution would not require the artist to abandon his work in order to become a husband, therefore, but rather to become a husband in order to become an artist. Neither Him nor Me, however, can love the other for what he or she really is, for neither knows him- or herself. He's worried that he's only an artist, and a poor one at that, while she's worried that she's only a wife and future mother. In reality, he is also her husband, just as she is also his lovely mistress. And yet, he's worried that she thinks of him only as a husband, while she's worried that he thinks of her only as a clever and intelligent woman. In reality, he senses and would like to accept her womanliness, just as she senses and would like to accept his artisthood. Their tragedy, then, as Maurer says, is one of cross-purposes, for they have become alienated from one another by a series of mutual misunderstandings, they

have erected walls between them which are not real, walls
which they themselves have created. For it is not necessary to separate dreaming from doing; they are different,
but mutually interdependent. A man must be himself
in order to transcend himself, he must love in order to
write. And a woman must be a woman in order to be a
mistress, a mistress in order to be a wife. To choose between opposites which are not alternatives is to choose
falsely.

The resolution, then, would require Him to love Me
as a mistress not in spite of her desire to become a wife
but rather because of it, and it would require Me to love
Him as a husband not in spite of his need to become an
artist but rather because of it. And, in order for this to
come about, each would have to know him- or herself,
and each would have to accept the other for what she or
he really is. This would require an openness and an
honesty to which neither has as yet attained, although the
play shows them struggling imperfectly toward it. If they
could achieve self-knowledge and self-acceptance, then
they would be able to understand and accept each other.
Let us turn now to the text in order to see how much light
this interpretation casts upon the play itself.

iv

Act One, Scene I. Doctor anesthetizing Me. The
three Weirds, rocking and knitting, are discussing tamed
hippopotami. This is nonsense, of course, but nonsense of
the highest order, for it is full of wit, satire, and wisdom
which casts an indirect light over the whole play. In their
serious and trivial domestic gossip, which is often built on
one *non sequitur* after another, they represent a comment
on the meaningless life of Cummings' mostpeople; the
surrealistic distortion serves a valid artistic purpose, for this
is what ordinary life is really like when seem clearly
through the artist's firsthand vision. And the artist's vision
is one of the things which this play is about. Its author's
Public said, we recall, "So far as I'm concerned, my very
dear sir, nonsense isn't everything in life," and he said this

because for him action is serious and dreaming is trivial. But what is serious to him is nonsense to the artist just because of the split between what is and what is desirable, fact and value. A devalued world *is* literally nonsensical, and hence nonsense is one of the artist's chief weapons against it, for by this means he can show it for what it really is.

Me's eyes close and the Doctor comes out with Him, whom he introduces to the three Miss Weirds as Mr. Anybody. Their names are Stop, Look, and Listen, and they react snobbishly until Him says he's really Everyman, Marquis de la Poussière (ironically, "Mr. Dust"). They are delighted to meet royalty, and, after the men leave, continue their previous chatter. The play on identities, the second thing which the play is about, should be obvious.

Scene II. The third term of the triad now becomes the central concern, as we see the first scene between the two lovers. The mirror wall of their room is the invisible one between players and audience. Me is primping at this mirror, complaining about her looks. Apparently, this is a sign of her pregnancy. Him, however, is writing, and attends to her rather absently. She's fretful and he's worried about his play, and this creates tension between them. She wants to break up, ostensibly because she realizes she's not clever; in actuality, we infer, she's worried about how he'll take the news of her condition and can't quite muster the courage to tell him. But she's not happy about the idea of breaking up, because "with part of you I think I'm in love" (p. 8). She tells him she's trying to decide something, and then she thinks he might already know, but again their purposes cross. Then she asks him to tell her about the play he's writing, but he evades her question by some witty biological double-talk about gametes and genes. Then he can hold himself in no longer, and tries to explain to her what being an artist means to him: "An artist, a man, a failure, MUST PROCEED" (pp. 12–13), although he tells her he is deeply involved in her. But again their moods diverge, she trying to apologise for her stupidity, and he trying to tell her "how much finer" she is than himself. I would guess that he's trying to tell her he isn't as confident in himself as she assumes: he told her previously, when she couldn't find her pocket mirror, "that it's safer to take your word for my looks" (p. 11). Being incomplete himself, not having learned who he is, he needs her love to give him the security he lacks in himself. The trouble is, of course, that she's not sure who *she* is either. Outside it's snowing; they talk of the circus, and they hear the sound of a drum. She sends him out to see what it is.

Scene III. The three Weirds chattering; Him enters. Nonsense. But the third makes some real sense, finally, saying: "Time is the autobiography of space. Give a woman everything and she has nothing. Life is a matter of being born. Treat a man like dirt and he will produce flowers. Art is a question of being alive.—Go in peace" (p. 19). In orphic form, these words comprise the paradoxical wisdom of love, life, and art which Him is struggling to learn. Thus do these crones fulfill their prophetic function as the three Fates.

Scene IV. The lovers' room, which has revolved clockwise one turn, so that the window wall is now the invisible space between players and audience. Him returns, and Me says he ought to write for money. He replies sarcastically, saying she looks terribly. She breaks down and cries, and he tries vainly to comfort her. She falls asleep on the couch, and he speaks to himself bitterly in the mirror, wondering why they can't understand one another. He'd like to kill the man in the mirror—because, we infer, that man is the part of him she loves, the husband part—and raises a pistol to his head. She wakes up in terror, and he tries to allay her fears by explaining that his "pistil" is only the "female organ of a flower" (p. 23). His biological doubletalk may cause her to assume he knows of her pregnancy, but she's not sure. At any rate, thinking he was in despair over their faltering love, she is enormously encouraged at what she takes to be his display of concern, and says she feels much better. She had previously thought he didn't care about her. Then they start discussing his battered old hat, and he betrays *his* doubts about *her*, for he doesn't think she cares about him. He tells her it's "the Other Man's hat," the Man in the Mirror, the one she really loves (the husband). As he shows her the mirror, however, she starts primping again and loses interest in what he's saying.

He then tries again to explain the artist's vision, and he does so in terms of the mirror and the window, objects which are gradually becoming the play's central symbols: "suppose that you are standing before a window and that continuously something happens—snow appears, covers the earth; melting, disappears—in other words, suppose that the earth rises, reappears, moves: suppose Spring. Or suppose that I am looking in a mirror and that my consciousness of the surface dissolves before an image as snow may melt before rain or as Winter melts before April and as the awake must dissolve before the asleep" (p. 28). Now it seems to me that the window may represent reality and the mirror may represent the imagination: what he's trying to say, then, is that at the heart of both is the secret of the organic world—growth, or, in a word, Spring—the outer and the inner worlds. He's trying to say that the window is a mirror and the mirror is a window, that truth and beauty, world and self, time and eternity, act and dream, is and ought, life and art are images of one another. But she looks out the window and can only see the snow. He reads from his notebook a passage describing the organicity of the world: "I do not stroke edges and I do not feel music but only metaphors. Metaphors are what comfort and astonish us, which are the projected brightness of ourselves—" (p. 29). The dynamic flux of the living reality, in other words, comes into being by means of the creative interchange between fact and mind, window and mirror: "There are no entities, no isolations, no abstractions; but there are departures, voyages, arrivals, contagions" (p. 28).

Again she fails to understand him, but asks what his play is all about. He replies, "This play of mine is all about mirrors," and his hero is the Man in the Mirror, a man "who is writing a play about a man who is writing a sort of a play" (pp. 29–30).

Scene V. The three Weirds chatter slogans and *non sequiturs* about sex, great men, and the biology of a certain species of fish.

Act Two, Scene I. The curtain rises and falls on a blank stage. The voices of Him and Me are heard discussing it. He says it's the Man in the Mirror's play (and hence, is not the one Him is writing). She asks him what this Other Play is all about, and he answers: "About? It's about anything you like, about nothing and something and everything, about blood and thunder and love and death — in fact, about as much as you can stand." He imagines an advertisement for it: "Broadway is enjoying a novel treat in one of the wittiest and most highly original products of American genius, entitled 'How Dyuh Get That Way?' By the authors of 'Nuf Ced' . . . the subject of this rollicking farce is the 18th Amendment; and right now we want to ask you, could anything be funnier?" (p. 35). The Eighteenth Amendment was, of course, the basis of Prohibition, but "How Dyuh Get That Way?" may have several meanings: it may be the amazed indignation of the playwright at the people he's portraying, or it may be that of the audience at the outrageousness of the play, or it may be both. At any rate, the remainder of Act Two consists of eight satirical scenes, with the doctor playing a leading role in each:

Scene II: Three drunken middle-aged men and a repressed old maid. *Scene III:* A snake oil vendor. *Scene IV:* Two business partners who have become each other. *Scene V:* A Censor tries to halt a bawdy performance of "Frankie and Johnie." *Scene VI:* An Englishman carrying his Unconscious is stopped by a detective. *Scene VII:* Two Babbitts aboard an ocean liner. *Scene VIII:* A burlesque "Roman" drama. *Scene IX:* A man is accosted by a hungry mob in the ruins of post-World War I Europe.

Several questions must be asked before the significance of this act can be interpreted. These eight scenes represent "a sample, taken at random" (p. 35) of the

Other Man's play. Why doesn't Him show Me some of his own play? Why is he showing her anything at all? Why, at the end of each scene, is she so unimpressed? What is the role of these scenes in the "plot" we have analyzed and interpreted? Answers must be sought in the nature of these scenes themselves. They are all farcical and satirical, except the last, which is painfully serious. Just before this last one appears, Me says, in response to the preceding "Roman" drama, "I hate history." And Him replies: "So do I.—Europe, Africa, Asia: continents of Give. America: the land of Keep—keep in step keep moving keep young keep your head keep in touch with events keep smiling keep your shirt on keep off the grass keep your arms and limbs inside the car" (pp. 73–74). Now it seems clear not only that the seven satirical scenes could have been written by Him rather than the Man in the Mirror, but also that they could have been written by Cummings himself. What I mean is that there is an obvious congruence among all three, whereas we have been led to believe that the Man in the Mirror was the Other Man, Him's rival, the husband-self he thinks Me loves and which he'd like to kill. If we were Him writing a play about his rival's play, wouldn't we try to show him up for the deadhead he really is? But what we have instead is a series of brilliant and mocking scenes, scenes which present a view of life which could only be Him's.

Now, either these scenes are there just for fun or they serve some purpose within the play. If the latter is the case, then the only reason I can think of is that Him told Me that this was the Other Man's play in order to throw her off the track, to get her interested. In reality, then, it is his play, but he tells her it's his rival's play in order to see if he can blend his two selves that way. For if he can get her to believe it's the Other Man's play, then he'll be able to show her that that's the way an artist sees the world too. And how is this world viewed? The way in which a transcendentalist sees the world of habit and routine—as a series of grotesques. And what has this to do with the "plot"? It's an attempt at self-definition by exclusion, and is somewhat similar to the process of writing satires which we commented on when discussing *is 5*: as if Cummings' values were being discovered negatively. Him, in other words, is trying to find out who he is by discovering who he is not.

But something is missing, and Me, at the end of each scene except the last, remains unimpressed. Him and Me do not discuss this scene at all, and it is ended by a curtain which concludes the entire act. And this is the scene which is serious rather than satirical, the one in which the "Gentleman" (played, of course, by the Doctor) learns that to be alive is to give—and this, as we know, is the same as to love. The result is that, at the end of Act Two, the Gentleman is just about to be born. All the preceding scenes had portrayed a world without love, and that is why Me remained unimpressed. Does this final scene mean, then, that Him is beginning to learn that to love equals to give? If so, then one more thing remains to be learned: that to give equals to be. Thus must Him pursue his quest for self-knowledge, the final and root-term of the triad, "love, art, and selftranscendence or growing."

Act Three, Scene I. The room has rotated once again, so that the door wall is the invisible one facing the audience. Him is making love to Me, but as usual their moods are far apart and she resists. He bitterly concludes she is truly the mistress of the Man in the Mirror, and she retorts by saying that she isn't the one *he* loves either. He wonders whether she is really having an affair with someone else, but she reassures him on that point. They see, however, that this is the end for them. She says he knows who he is, but that she doesn't know who she is. And then all his insecurity bursts forth: "All my life I've wondered if I'm any good. If my head and my heart are made out of something firmer or more living than what I see everywhere covering itself with hats and with linen" (p. 95). And this is the root, I think, of the trouble between them: that a person cannot give himself in love until he has first found himself. Him says he envies her, "That you are something which I supremely would like to discover:

knowing that it exists in itself as I do not exist and as I never have existed. How do I know this? Because through you I have come to understand that whatever I may have been or may have done is mediocre. (*Bitterly*) You have made me realize that in the course of living I have created several less or more interesting people—none of whom was myself" (pp. 95–96). A man who doesn't know himself cannot love, and a man who cannot love cannot be an artist. She concludes, however, that she doesn't know what he's like either, and says it's better to break up. We may infer, as Maurer does, that she thinks she knows what *she's* like and she thinks that this is not what he wants, and that therefore she is mistakenly freeing him for his art just at the moment when he is trying to tell her he was mistaken about the supposed opposition between art and love.

Scene II: The three Weirds chattering about guinea pigs having children. *Scene III:* Him has gone to Paris, and we find him in a restaurant in the midst of a scene which is very much like the satirical scenes in Act Two from the Other Man's play. We may infer, I think, that without Me, he is now actually living in the loveless world he merely wrote about before. As his art failed, so now his life fails: he has entered the world of his art and finds it flat and sour to the taste. *Scene IV:* The three Weirds garble domestic trivialities and commercial slogans. The Doctor's head has left the picture, Me's eyes open slowly, and the Doctor's head reappears to shout insults at the crones.

Scene V. The room has rotated once again, so that the solid wall is now the invisible one facing the audience. Him has returned, and we learn from his conversation with Me how they met again quite by accident one rainy day (it is apparently spring by now). After an awkward afternoon at their old apartment, he had gone down to the Battery (?) and there had met a man with green eyes. This was, we infer, his double, his other self, and one of them killed the other—he can't remember which. Is Him still thinking in terms of opposites which aren't alternatives?

Or is his confusion a sign that his two halves are blending together? But *something* has happened to him since he went away, for he feels like Rip Van Winkle returning from a long sleep. They begin talking a bit regretfully about the possibility of having made a mistake, but she isn't clear as to what mistake he means. Then he tells her about a dream he had, a dream about a baby daughter. This would seem to be his confession that he wants to be a husband and father, but she, apparently having mistaken their talk about making mistakes—thinking perhaps that he meant it was a mistake to have married her in the first place—puts him off. He talks about his childhood and about how one loses one's illusions. Then they hear a drum sounding. The scene is concluded with his bitter regret that he has failed to reconcile truth and beauty. He cannot believe his devotion to art has shut hum from reality and self-knowledge: "How should what is desirable shut us entirely from what is? No! That must be not quite all: I will not think that the tragedy can be so simple. There must be something else: I believe that there IS something else: and my heart tells me that unless I discover this now I will never discover it" (p. 130). And this is as far as he can go—to realize the nature of the problem, but not to discover its solution: that art depends upon love and love upon self-knowledge, that they are mutually interdependent rather than mutually exclusive. The drumsound gets louder and the voice of a circus barker ends the scene.

Scene VI. The barker, who is the Doctor in disguise, introduces each of nine freaks (one for each month of Me's pregnancy). The spectators are all the characters from Act II and the three Miss Weirds. The ninth and last freak is Princess Anankay (the goddess of Necessity and the mother of the three Fates), who turns out to be Me holding a newborn babe in her arms. The three Weirds cry, "It's all done with mirrors!" and Him utters a cry of terror at the sight. Blackout. What can all this mean in terms of the whole? I think three worlds are intersecting here at once: the sterile world of Him's play, the world of the lovers, and a third and new world—that of the freaks. And I think that each world is meant to complement the other, thereby remedying the inner lack of each. We know Cummings' admiration for the circus, and we may recall Him's having told Me how he feels about the freakshow: "I seem to remember riding out of a circus once upon a time on somebody's shoulder; and hearing a throbbing noise, and then a coarse voice squirting a stream of bright words—and looking, and seeing a small tent with huge pictures of all sorts of queer things, and the barker spieling like a fiend, and people all about him gaping like fish. Whereupon, I began to tremble—and begged somebody to take me in; which somebody probably did, I don't remember" (p. 16). I think these freaks, then, represent life and vitality to Him. Would it be too much to say that, as the ordinary world looks grotesque to the artist, so too do real individuals look like freaks to the ordinary world? Thus the final freak of all, a woman and her baby, causes the crowd to recoil and the Misses Weird to turn up their noses in disgust.

Why, then, does Him utter "a cry of terror" (p. 144)? Because he is still caught in his own dilemma: the world of Me and her baby has entered the world of his art and has transformed it—for this is what was missing—and yet he has been unable to effect this transformation within himself. This interpretation is borne out by the final scene.

Scene VII. The room is now back where it started, with the invisible mirror between the play and the audience. But the mirror has become a window, as Me discovers, for she suddenly realizes that there are real people in the audience and that they are pretending that this room and its occupants are real. Thus have art and life, play and audience, intersected. But Him can't believe it, and so remains to the very end frozen in the dilemma whose meaning he is just beginning to understand.

v

We are now in a position to assess the value of Cummings' technical experiments in this play, for they seem clearly to function organically in relation to the "plot." This plot is about the relation between art and life, and the problem of identity and self-knowledge, and so the various devices which attempt to bring audience and play closer together, and to set up mirroring effects, seem wholly appropriate and effective. Maurer feels that much of the surrealistic effect may be accounted for by the theory that the play is Me's dream while under anesthesia. This explains why the Doctor is the master of illusion, for he is administering the anesthetic. It may also explain the man-writing-a-play-about-a-man-writing-a-play trick, for the Doctor is the hero of the Other Man's play, who is the hero of Him's play (who is the hero of Cummings' plays!)

But this seems too gimmicky to me, and I feel a better explanation is found, as I hope I have shown, in the necessities of the plot itself. The distortions, in other words, grow out of the play's meanings and not just out of another framing device. The scenes of Act II, for example, are not grotesque because they are being dreamed by Me, but rather because (1) they represent a play within a play, and so demand separate treatment (cf. the deliberate stiffness of the acting in *Hamlet*'s play within a play), and (2) they illustrate how the ordinary world looks to the transcendental vision of the artist (as well as satirize, incidentally, a variety of popular dramatic styles).

A few words should be said about Cummings' style in this play. And it is impressive indeed, ranging all the way from the coarse colloquial speech of the barker to the lyrical beauty of some of the lovers' scenes. In between is the everyday talk of the lovers, for all its misunderstandings, with its delicacy, its grace, and especially its accuracy. The really puzzling thing about this play is not its difficulty or its undeserved neglect, but rather its uniqueness. I don't understand why Cummings didn't develop and exploit this brilliant dramatic vein further.

Regarding its significance in the framework of Cummings' growth, two things should be noted: the maturing of his conception of love, and the frank presentation of the artist's self-doubt. This last point deserves special notice, for it refutes the charge that Cummings' work is marred by arrogance, and it also helps to explain it. Since knowledge of oneself is one of the bases of art for Cummings, self-doubt is not a virtue. Yet that does not mean he always had such knowledge, and this work represents a crucial transitional stage for him. In struggling to find himself in his art, he finds he lacks the ability to give himself in love, and so he must find out who he is before he can be either artist or lover.

Let us trace his development further, then.

VIVA (1931), **NO THANKS** (1935),
       NEW POEMS (1938)

WE START a new decade with Cummings' values becoming crystallized and his long search for a language and an instrument in which to embody them achieving its direction. For as we shall see, the most notable development to be found in his first book of poems of the thirties is the full-fledged appearance of a characteristic conceptual vocabulary. And I suspect that this development has something to do with the struggle which is represented in *Him*: such terms as "now" and "because" were used in the play as nouns, and his grasp of the relation between love and art in terms of the transcendental vision was becoming more certain.

I have read somewhere that "ViVa" (Cummings' title actually consists of two interlocking capital "V's" — W) was the motto of the Italian Fascists of the thirties, but if this is true it should be clear that there is nothing political in Cummings' use of the term. His view of democracy may be sometimes hostile, but his view of totalitarianism is even more hostile, and no apologies are needed on this score. The obvious interpretation is the best: he means to say, by this title, "Live!" The book contains seventy poems numbered consecutively, and they are not grouped or divided in any way. They may, however, be classified in six groups as follows:

1] Satires — contains ten poems. These attack routinized humanity, science, U. S. political hypocrisy, utopianisms, big business, certain classes of writers, and the military

(I, VII, XIII, XVII, XX, XXII, XXIV, XXVI, XXVII, XXX). The satirical vision, having emerged clearly in *is 5*, has now become a standard part of Cummings' outlook, and I feel here that it is a bit more focused. The War and the Depression left their mark on his view of things, and he is becoming more certain of the enemy. Thus the targets here are more specific: Taft, Wilson, McKinley, Teddy Roosevelt, Coolidge, Hutchinson, Mussolini, Marx, Darwin, Harding, and so on. What bothers him in these poems, of course, is the way in which the planners and politicians are trying to put a broken world back together without love.

2] Comedies—contains three poems: a sexual joke, the portrait of Miss Gay, and some fun about a Chinese sage and a vibrant young girl (XII, XVIII, XXXII). Further comment would be superfluous.

3] The Poet and his City—contains ten poems. These portray barroom vignettes, street scenes, city people, and incidents of the day (II, IV, V, VI, IX, X, XIX, XXI, XXIII, XLV). This is Cummings' demimonde, and his interest in belly dancers is matched by his interest in bums, tramps, and gangsters. Indeed, it is hard to avoid reading VI symbolically (a226–27):

> but mr can you maybe listen there's
> me &
> some people
> and others please
> don't
> confuse. . . .

Both the panhandler and the artist view middle-class society from the outside, and critics who say Cummings is being inconsistent in satirizing the politicians who would help these very hoboes he sympathizes with are entirely missing the point. Indeed, it is the same point which they miss in complaining about his treatment of the Negro: it is not social welfare and bourgeois status these people need. In most of the important ways, they are better off the way they are—at least they are honest and alive—and he likes them for what they are. The mistake is for the Reformer to try to make the tramp respectable, the Negro white. They are the few remaining flies in the bland and homogenized ointment of a sterile society, and the poet identifies with them as such.

4] Impressions—contains nine poems. Sunsets, moons, stars, and spring are the subjects here (XI, XXXI, XXXVI, XXXVII, XXXVIII, XXXIX, XL, XLI, XLVI). Experimental and typographical techniques, which are now becoming more frequent, are used most often in the satirical and comic poems for mockery and violence, and in the city and descriptive poems for movement and vision.

5] Love and Lovers—contains twenty-seven poems (nineteen various pieces—XIV, XV, XLIV, XLVII–LXII—plus eight sonnets—LXIII–LXX). We noted in *is 5* the tentative emergence of a transcendental treatment of love, and one of the crucial things in *ViVa* is the gradual strengthening of this treatment in at least half a dozen poems, especially in some of the love sonnets. Consider LXIII, for example (a267–68 *):

be unto love as rain is unto colour;create
me gradually(or as these emerging now
hills invent the air)
            breathe simply my each how
my trembling where my still unvisible when.   Wait

if i am not heart,because at least i beat
—always think i am gone like a sun which must go
sometimes,to make an earth gladly seem firm for you:
remember(as those pearls more than surround this throat)
i wear your dearest fears beyond their ceaselessness

(nor has a syllable of the heart's eager dim
enormous language loss or gain from blame or praise)
but many a thought shall die which was not born of dream
while wings welcome the year and trees dance(and i guess

though wish and world go down,one poem yet shall swim

There are many foreshadowings of the mature love poetry here, although the artistic and emotional discipline and control of later years are somewhat lacking. Notice the metaphorical equation at the beginning, what Lloyd Frankenberg was to call "the algebra of the heart." Notice also the parallelisms in the syntax: "be-create-breathe-wait-think-remember," "my each how-my trembling where-my still unvisible when," and "loss or gain from blame or praise." Notice finally the verbs and adverbs made into nouns: "how," "where," "when," and "dream."

Although the speaker is urging his lady to love him, the point is that he is doing so not in the traditional threatening or pleading manner but rather in a consoling or reassuring way. She is apparently afraid, we may infer, of the losses which will follow upon her complete surrender, and she is afraid of not arousing in him a full response. Now those losses which she fears are not the traditional ones referring to chastity and virginity either, but are rather transcendental ones, the ones lost when the ordinary world and its empty values are scorned—hopes, ambitions, successes. The speaker's problem, then, is to show her she has nothing to fear.

Thus he begins by assuring her that he is waiting, ready to respond to her—that his manner, his place, and his time will come into being as she breathes. If he seems unready, it is because he has gone like the sun—only to return—and he tells her to remember that he wears her fears (as she wears a necklace of pearls) beyond the point of their apparent endlessness—that is, that he occupies an angle of vision from which ceaseless fears no longer appear ceaseless. The "heart's eager dim/ enormous language" refers, I think, to art, specifically to poetry, and it is at this point that the relationship between art and love emerges. This language, he tells her, exists beyond the ordinary categories of praise or blame, for nothing in the world of routine can add to or subtract from it. Thoughts born in that world, on the other hand, are tied to it and will therefore die when it dies, while the natural world, the world of process and becoming, continues to be reborn. He concludes by telling her that one poem at least will survive the destruction of the ordinary world.

What is the chain of reasoning here? That she should not fear his remoteness because it is due to his transcendental vision, and that this vision is capable of producing one immortal poem. She can breathe him back into the mortal world by her love, and he can make of that love a song out of the "heart's language." She is, finally, to forget her fears—that he is not of this world, and that this world is painful to lose—and place her trust in him and his art. If art is a mystery, we recall, it is love which is the mystery of mysteries, and the lover here has moved well beyond the hero of *Him* in the latter's unsuccessful struggle to unite an artist's vision with a man's love.

6] Poems of Praise—contains two poems. The first is an admiring portrait of a man who has the transcendental vision (XXXV), and the second is a loving description of his mother and father in heaven (XLIII). This tentative beginning turns out ultimately to develop into a genre, for Cummings applauds as much as he decries. There are in addition nine poems which I find either difficult to interpret or unclassifiable (III, VIII, XVI, XXV, XXVIII, XXIX, XXXIII, XXXIV, XLII).

But the really significant achievement of *ViVa* is not so much the emergence of the transcendental vision as the forging of a style for its expression. The problem, as we have seen, is to counteract the abstract tendency of language, and the solution is to make nouns out of verbs, adverbs, adjectives, and so on, thereby preserving motion in the midst of stasis, structure in the midst of function (a252–53, no. XLII):

> structure,miraculous challenge,devout am
>
> upward deep most invincible unthing
> —stern sexual timelessness,outtowering
> this noisy impotence of not and same
>
> answer,beginning,ecstasy,to dare:

I call this a "conceptual" vocabulary because Cummings uses it to express ideas, but they are ideas which are at bottom inexpressible, and so they can only be suggested by means of grammatical shifts, a kind of metaphor. The kernel of meaning is clear, but the connotative range is wide. These ideas and this vocabulary seem to me to be prominent in about twenty-three poems of this volume, and they cut across the other categories, although they seem to be mainly in the Impressions and Lovers Groups. Transcendentalism, that is, and its diction have naturally to do with nature's changes—spring, twilight, star, moon, sunset, dawn—and with love; with the process of becoming, and with the surrender requisite to its perception (VIII, XIX, XXXIV, XXXV, XXXIX, XL, XLI, XLII, XLIII, XLIV, XLVIII, LII, LIII, LIV, LV, LVIII, LIX, LXI, LXII, LXIII, LXIV, LXVIII, LXIX—some of these use the conceptual vocabulary in a comic or satirical way as well). Perhaps as a result of the development of such a vocabulary, the style of this volume as a whole is less redundantly flamboyant than hitherto, less excited and more controlled.

ii

As if needing time to extend his discoveries regarding transcendentalism and its language, Cummings in the next four years devotes almost one-third of his poems explicitly to treating and mastering the problems involved. This fact, plus a resurgence of interest in the possibilities of typographical experimentation, are the distinguishing marks of *No Thanks*. But that is to get a bit ahead of our story.

The title refers, of course, to the fact that the manuscript was rejected by fourteen publishers, those whose names are listed on the dedication page (it was finally published by the Golden Eagle Press). This is a curious and embarrassing problem, for Cummings had already published no fewer than nine books, two of which (*No Title* and *Eimi*) had been published by Covici, Friede, one of the now hostile fourteen. Most of the hostile ones were and still are among the top houses, one of which— Harcourt, Brace—was later to bring out *Collected Poems*

(1938), *Poems 1923–1954* (1954), and 95 *Poems* (1958). It would appear that Cummings' other publishers up to this point—Boni and Liveright, The Dial Press, and Thomas Seltzer—were either no longer receptive, no longer solvent, or defunct. At any rate, the truth seems to be that in 1935—thirteen years after the appearance of his first book—Cummings' work was still too controversial to attract a major publisher.

No Thanks contains seventy-one numbered poems and they are not further subdivided, but they may be grouped in a way similar to that in which *ViVa* was grouped.

1] Satires—contains fourteen poems. The targets here are a captain of industry, mostpeople, a United States president throwing a baseball, Santa Claus haters, band-waggoners, utopian reformers, the average American, literary iconoclasts, Hemingway, famous fatheads, Communists, and so on (6, 8, 9, 15, 21, 22, 23, 24, 26, 28, 29, 30, 54, 55). I think the dangers of a mass society are becoming clearer in Cummings' mind, and this in the middle of the thirties, well in advance of our anxious post-World War II prosperity with its host of viewers-with-alarm, such as Fromm, Riesman, Packard *et al.* Consider number 23, for example (a292–93):

> *he does not have to feel because he thinks*
> *(the thoughts of others,be it understood).* . . .

If Freud drew upon the poets for some of his insights, then the social critics of the fifties either did or could have drawn similarly on Cummings. It seems to me that the concept of other-directedness was anticipated by twenty years in this poem. Or look at number 54 (a314):

> *while Gadgets murder squawk and add,*
> *the cult of Same is all the chic* . . .

or at number 55 (a314–15):

> *worshipping Same*
> *they squirm and they spawn*
> *and a world is for them,them;whose*
> *death's to be born)* . . .

Before fish-tailed automobiles, deep-freezers, television, and automatic computers, Cummings saw the straws in the wind. If it is natural to think of him as a critic of mass society, it is not so common to realize how early some of these poems were written. It may even be that they have outlived their own success, for we are so used to such criticism nowadays that we are likely to take these satires simply for granted.

2] Comedies—contains four poems: a pair of sexual jokes, a telephone conversation, and a play on the proverb about going to the ant (16, 17, 18, 20).

3] The City—contains three poems (4, 5, 60). What is of special significance here is the gradual disappearance of the demimonde from the poet's interests, for there are practically no poems of this type in the remaining five books of poetry. Perhaps the world of bars, dancehalls, prostitutes, and gangsters belongs in reality to the poet's college and war years—and especially to the twenties—and therefore fades as those years fade. I would guess also that their fading has some connection with the poet's growth, as Cummings is now forty-one and becoming more interested in other things.

4] Impressions—contains sixteen poems. There is a growing interest, for example, in trying to weave typographical nets to ensnare the moon, the snow, the night, spring, stars, birds, grasshoppers, mice, and so on (1, 2, 13, 14, 33, 34, 38, 40, 46, 51, 52, 53, 57, 59, 63, 70). The importance which Cummings attaches to this type of poem —many of which are vertical, like the legends on Japanese prints—is indicated by the fact that he has placed one of them at the head of almost every volume of poetry since No Thanks (Xaipe is the sole exception). And I think their importance is not yet fully appreciated, for if what I have said about the relation between Cummings' transcendentalism, his view of nature, and his theory of technique is correct, then these poems should be seen as having central significance and not as being merely obsessive typographical doodlings. They are not jokes, much less are they poetic trivia: if the transcendental vision is achieved when

nature's dynamic process is glimpsed, then these typo-
graphs are the means by which such glimpses may be
passed on to the reader. It is as if the poet were looking
for ways to hand us a brimming cup without spilling any
of the wine: his breath is held and his hand moves very
slowly. We should not be fooled either by the smallness
of the subject or the unorthodoxy of the technique, for it
is not so much the subject which is important as the fact
that it is in motion, and it is not so much the technique
which is important as the fact that it aims at creating
movement. What we have here, in fact, is a unique Cummings genre, a combination of the English-American
Imagist poem, the Japanese Haiku, and Coleridge's meta-
physics (a307, no. 46 *):

        swi(
            across!gold's

        rouNdly
)ftblac
        kl(ness)y

        a-motion-upo-nmotio-n

        Less?
           thE
        (against
        is
)Swi

        mming

        (w-a)s
        bIr

        d,

This poem is made up of two parts—one outside the
parentheses, and the other inside. The first is the noun-
adjective part, while the second is the verb-adverb part:
"swift blackly, a motion upon motionless, the swimming

bird" tells us *what,* while "across gold's roundlyness, against is-was" tells us *where.* The point is, of course, that this bird is moving, moving simultaneously across the sun (space) and against is-was (time), and hence for the speaker represents a living moment of perception, an instant of motion. Now, the problem is to catch that instant without freezing it in a static frame; to fix and print, as it were, a motion picture without losing the motion. This is done by breaking words, interlacing phrases, punctuating at odd points, capitalizing in the midst of words, and coining words. Critics who say the same effects can be created by conventional means must bear the burden of proof, realizing first of all just what the effect is that Cummings is aiming at, and secondly showing what the alternatives are for achieving it.

Indeed, Cummings has found and developed in this book four or five new devices in addition. Certain poems, for example, appear to have a more obvious visual shape than has been customary (43, 47, 59). Then there are the poems, furthermore, in which words are interlaced (20, 52, 53, 59, 63); those in which capital letters appear and disappear (1, 70); and those in which words are built by cumulative increments (40, 63, 70). And there are the satires, finally, in which comic effects are created by the use of spelling puns (22, 28, 30). "Never to rest and never to have: only to grow."

5] Transcendental poems—contains twenty-three poems, fourteen of which are sonnets (the sonnets are 3, 7, 11, 19, 31, 35, 37, 41, 45, 49, 61, 65, 69, 71, and the others are 10, 36, 39, 50, 58, 62, 66, 67, 68). The really significant development in this book, as I have already suggested, is the large and clear group of poems devoted not so much to subjects having transcendental aspects as to transcendentalism as a subject in itself. There seems to be a kind of climax of development here: as love was finally seen within its true transcendental framework in ViVa, so is transcendentalism itself (often combined, however, with love) now the major concern. Hereinafter transcendental statement will resume its normal subsidiary place as a part rather than as the whole in any given poem. Let us look more closely at one of the sonnets (a282–83, no. 1 *):

sonnet entitled how to run the world)

A always don't there B being no such thing
for C can't casts no shadow D drink and

E eat of her voice in whose silence the music of spring
lives F feel opens but shuts understand
G gladly forget little having less

with every least each most remembering
H highest fly only the flag that's furled

(sestet entitled grass is flesh or swim
who can and bathe who must or any dream
means more than sleep as more than know means guess)

I item i immaculately owe
dying one life and will my rest to these

children building this rainman out of snow

I would guess that the nine isolated capitals are visual merely and are not to be pronounced, for they don't appear to fit the meter. Their function would seem to be to create a kind of mock-agenda format, along with the two "entitled's" and the "item," parodying those who think the world needs some kind of program. For Cummings is saying the ordinary world and its sterile rules ("can't") doesn't exist ("casts no shadow"). The alternative is to partake of the earth and her changes, for she is real; the heart opens her mysteries, but the intellect closes them. Surrender, he says, what little the ordinary world has to offer, realizing that those with the transcendental vision have even less of worldly attachments. "Less," as well as "least each most," are paradoxical-ironic terms, meaning that the less one is attached to this world the more he is in tune with the transcendental one. Cummings frequently plays with these and similar terms of degree, with their comparatives and superlatives, as a way of making and intensifying the distinction between the two worlds. I doubt whether "with every least each most remembering" has any specific paraphrasable meaning, but I suspect it suggests something such as "with each least memory of the world of habit and each most memory of the world of insight," or "with each intensest memory, the smallest as well as the largest." At any rate, he says we should, with each memory, try to fly only the furled flag highest, the application being that pride in worldly things must be trimmed if we are to rise to the transcendent vision. The sestet has three suggested titles: "grass is flesh" (nature is alive), or "swim who can and bathe who must" (let those who can achieve the transcendent vision achieve it, and those who can't fail), or "any dream/ means more than sleep [,] as more than know means guess" (just as intuition grasps the transcendent vision more than intellect does, so too does dreaming mean more than simply sleeping). He concludes, in Yeatsian fashion, by making his will, reversing the usual "I owe life one death" and implying thereby that life in the ordinary world is merely an episode in the larger scheme of natural cycles. What is left over—that is, everything—is willed to a group of children making a snowman in the rain (or perhaps they are making a snowman which is melting into rain as they build, snow being the crystallized form of rain and vice versa, so that this phrase implies a dynamic state somewhere in between), for they are young and innocent and can still take pleasure in making something for the fun of it. Children, like tramps and Negroes and showpeople, are akin to the artist in this routineless approach to life.

6] Praise—contains six poems. Here are the alternatives to "this death named Smith"—"Married and lies/ afraid; aggressive and:American" (a292–93, no. 23). They are Joe Gould, Sally Rand, Negroes, the real proletariat, Paul Draper, and the image of the poet (27, 42, 43, 44, 48, 56). Number 44 is especially interesting, for it appears only in the holograph edition of *No Thanks*. The reason is obviously because it contains some four-letter obscenities, but I wish it could be reprinted for it is a rollicking and bawdy poem of great delight. It begins:

> *The boys i mean are not refined*
> *they go with girls who buck and bite. . . .*

and it concludes:

> *they speak whatever's on their mind*
> *they do whatever's in their pants*
> *the boys i mean are not refined*
> *they shake the mountains when they dance*

Four poems remain which I find obscure or hard to classify (12, 25, 32, 64).

iii

The well-known and popular *Collected Poems* of 1938 is in reality misnamed, for it contains a bit less than three-quarters of the poems published in book form up to that time. It does, however, take a fair sample from each of the preceding six volumes (*Tulips and Chimneys, &, XLI Poems, is 5, ViVa,* and *No Thanks*), and it includes, in addition to an Introduction, twenty-two new poems. *Poems 1923–1954*, then, appropriately represents this volume as "New Poems [from Collected Poems] (1938)," and gives the Introduction and the twenty-two new poems.

The Introduction (a331–32) is worth pausing over, for in it Cummings decided to explain the transcendental vision he had been discovering in his poetry. He had been twenty-six years old when he wrote his essay on Lachaise, and he was now forty-four. Eighteen years had passed, and he was apparently ready for an interim report. He was to produce another interim report in his "Foreword to Krazy" eight years later, and a third in *i:six nonlectures* seven years after that. It is a pity that Cummings' prose pieces were not more readily available until recently, and it is a shame that his critics have not paid more attention to those that *were* available.

The prose of this Introduction is unlike that of the Lachaise essay, with its young analytical exuberance, or of the "Foreword to Krazy," with its mature mystical logic, or of *six nonlectures*, with its aged and luminous clarity. The prose here is poetic, vivid, urgent, rising to a fiery jet of intensity, and subsiding on a brilliant note of ultimate affirmation of mystery. Cummings begins by distinguishing between the minority of human beings (you and I) and the majority of snobs (mostpeople). Let's not pretend, he says, that they are the same. Now, although this appears to be a kind of reverse snobbism in itself, it is important to notice that Cummings is anxious to include as many people as possible in the class of human beings. The implication is that, since he is trying to write for human beings, anyone who reads this book—or any poet's book—is a human being. Any charge of snobbism, then, must be based not on the fact that he leaves us out but rather on the fact that he includes himself in. That the world is divided between those who are trying to remain responsive and those who have surrendered to routine can, I think, hardly be denied. Thus the issue hinges upon the question of who belongs in which class. If it is egoism to distinguish between these two classes, then Cummings is an egoist; if it is snobbism to place oneself in the first class, then Cummings is a snob. But I would rather call it honesty, for he has by now found and taken his stand: there are some things which are, even for an eternal questioner, beyond question. Him was horrified at the possibility that he might be the same as everybody else; apparently Cummings, eleven years later, has allayed those doubts once and for all.

The only real objection, as I see it, is the implication that if you don't like these poems then you are not a human being. But the fact that Cummings goes on for over a page to explain the difference between human beings and snobs contradicts this inference. What he does next, therefore, is to list the defining traits of each class, and it is according to these and not the poems that we may decide where we belong—he does not decide for us. "Take the

matter of being born," for example. Mostpeople regard
their entrance into the natural world of cycles as a trau-
matic experience, an insult, a catastrophe. They are snobs
in the sense that they think they are too good for this
messy world of dynamic process; they prefer stasis and
safety instead. Human beings, on the other hand, "can
never be born enough," for "birth is a supremely welcome
mystery,the mystery of growing." And we grow only when
we remain our natural, first-hand, responsive selves, when
we see and feel for ourselves, when we avoid becoming
someone else, for this is "the mystery which happens only
and whenever we are faithful to ourselves." This means
that we live in the timeless eternity of the perpetual present, alive at every point to the pressure of the moment.

And what are the characteristic outlooks which distinguish human beings from mostpeople? For the latter, life
is a secondhand abstraction made by science and sold by
advertising. In this view, everything fits into predeter-
mined categories: a mountain is dead and a mammal is
alive, for they are separate orders of being. Luckily for
human beings, however, "a mountain is a mammal": life
is process, nature is alive, and the world is a metaphor.
The trouble is, though, that a genuine human being (an
artist, for example) looks to mostpeople like a ghost, because he doesn't live in what they consider to be the real
world. But he is genuinely alive—and here Cummings
grows rhapsodic in describing him: "The now of his each
pitying free imperfect gesture. . . ."

He concludes by explaining the uncategorized world of
his poems: "Miracles are to come. . . . nothing proving
or sick or partial. Nothing false,nothing difficult or easy
or small or colossal. . . . Never the murdered finalities
of wherewhen and yesno,impotent nongames of wrong-
right and rightwrong;never to gain or pause,never the soft
adventure of undoom,greedy anguishes and cringing ecstasies of inexistence;never to nest and never to have:only
to grow.

"Always the beautiful answer who asks a more beautiful
question." This is the transcendental world of becoming,

as opposed to the habitual world of routine; categories of space and time, as well as moral and legal categories, falsify the true nature of reality with an overlay—like the cellophane covering a wedding cake—of abstractions. In the world of becoming, all is fluid and dynamic, it is a world of questions; in the world of habit, all is static and fixed, it is a world of answers. As Cummings was to write six years later, in 1 × 1 (a404, no. XXVI *):

> when god decided to invent
> everything he took one
> breath bigger than a circustent
> and everything began
>
> when man determined to destroy
> himself he picked the was
> of shall and finding only why
> smashed it into because

One problem remains: it might be thought that Cummings does, in spite of his insistence on a world apart from categories, divide the world up into human beings and mostpeople, good and bad, yes and no, and so on. Does not the result contradict the intention? I don't think so, for he did not create this division; it was created for him—in *The Enormous Room*, and later in *Eimi*. But one does not need to be thrown into a concentration camp or go to Russia in order to see that the world is divided between dead habit and living responsiveness. The poet who sees an uncategorized world is not contradicting himself by criticizing the categorized world, so long as that categorized world keeps insisting that it exists. The poet of organic nature is not by that token a poet without values: to say that he denies our moral categories is not to say that he has no morality. For Cummings is the most moral of poets, and he attaches value to sensation only when sensation truly reveals insight into the organic life of the world. To value flux and process may be a paradox, but it is not a contradiction; to make a principle out of having no fixed principles is a puzzle only to the sophist, and to try to embody the concrete in abstract language is a bother only to the Philistine who wants to know precisely where he is at all times and therefore ends up nowhere.

Let us see, then, into what groups the twenty-two new poems may be divided (here too the categories are not fixed, but are used only for the convenience of discussing the poems in some intelligible way):

1] Satires and Comedies—contains eight poems. The subjects here are a learned astronomer (cf. Whitman), sick tourists on a ship, the utopian idea, the English, a wedding cake, conformity, movie makers, and a sexual joke (2, 3, 4, 6, 8, 11, 12, 14).

2] Impressions—contains five poems. Here are described people in fog, a moon, a snow scene, rain in the spring, and birds in the fall (1, 7, 10, 20, 21).

3] Transcendental Values—contains six poems. In these poems Cummings opposes laughter to money, human generosity to social problems, fisherman to scientists, stars and trees to abstractions, openness to categories, and decries the idea of economic security (5, 13, 15, 16, 18, 19).

4] Love—contains two poems (17, 22). The second one is worth looking at more closely, for in it Cummings seems to be returning to the transcendental treatment of love he discovered in ViVa (a345 *):

> you shall above all things be glad and young.
> For if you're young,whatever life you wear
>
> it will become you;and if you are glad
> whatever's living will yourself become.
> Girlboys may nothing more than boygirls need:
> i can entirely her only love
>
> whose any mystery makes every man's
> flesh put space on;and his mind take off time
>
> that you should ever think,may god forbid
> and (in his mercy) your true lover spare:
> for that way knowledge lies,the foetal grave
> called progress,and negation's dead undoom.

* Copyright, 1938, by E. E. Cummings and reprinted by permission of Harcourt, Brace & World, Inc.

> *I'd rather learn from one bird how to sing*
> *than teach ten thousand stars how not to dance*

This sonnet has many of the marks of Cummings' fully mature love poetry: the regularity of its progress, the balance of its lines and ideas, its clear transcendentalism, its use of a characteristic conceptual vocabulary, its sense of mastery and control, its distortion of syntax, and so on. Perhaps one or two points call for comment, however. The fifth line has always puzzled me, but I think it means "girlboys may need nothing more than boygirls," in the sense that ordinary lovers—those whose identity is confused and indistinct—may need nothing more than ordinary people to love. If this is so, then a "but" must be inferred at the beginning of the sixth line, and lines six to eight would read: "but I can entirely love her only whose mystery breaks down the usual categories and brings a man's body and mind thereby into the transcendental world." That would explain the persuasions of the first four lines, for if she becomes glad and young, his lady will contain such a mystery—she and life (livingness) will become the same. The concluding sextet, then, continues this line of argument by condemning reason, the maker of categories, in favor of organic reality (the bird's song).

5] Praise—contains one poem (9). This is a celebration dedicated to the dancer, Jimmy Savo, one of the many performers whose nimble art Cummings has loved.

6 ANTHROPOS (1930), NO TITLE (1930), TOM (1935)

IN SPITE of the oft-repeated complaint that Cummings' work is too repetitive, the fact is that, outside the poetry at least, he rarely does the same thing twice. *Eimi* only remotely resembles *The Enormous Room*, *Him* and *Santa Claus* are poles apart as plays, and *No Title* and *Tom* are altogether unique. And yet, it seems to me, each represents a significant achievement; there must be in Cummings a certain prodigality of talent and energy which allows him to try such a variety of forms, put all he has into each, and then go on to the next. Of course, each is not equally significant or equally successful: I think *Him* is unsurpassable, and *The Enormous Room* is a perennial favorite; I have great respect for *Eimi*, and I like *Santa Claus* very much; but *Anthropos*, *No Title*, and *Tom* are much slighter things by comparison. Let us see what they have to offer.

Published in book form in 1944, *Anthropos: or The Future of Art* first appeared in 1930 in an anthology edited by Walter S. Hankel called *Whither, Whither, or After Sex, What? A Symposium to End Symposiums*. It occupies some thirteen pages in this anthology, but in book form it takes up about twenty-five pages. Although I have not seen the anthology, I doubt whether Cummings made any changes, for the 1944 edition is a beautifully designed book in which the number of lines per page gradually increases and diminishes as the play unfolds. This would explain the apparent increase in size. My study, then, is based on the 1944 book.

Less a play than an exemplum or skit, *Anthropos* in some respects anticipates *Santa Claus*. The three politicians are Death, the artist is Santa Claus, and the mob is the mob. Although it is printed without formal divisions, the action falls into three parts:

1] The scene, which remains the same throughout, is the inside of a cave. On the left are three infrahuman creatures dressed in filthy skins, on the right is a naked man drawing something on the wall, and in the central background is a curtain of skins behind which is heard the noise of a machine clanking. The action consists of two parts proceeding simultaneously: the three creatures are discussing something while the artist is constructing his design, neither side paying attention to the other. The three creatures, who are named "G," "O," and "D" respectively, are trying, in the twentieth-century vernacular, to hit upon the proper slogan—for what purpose, we don't as yet know—and they are considering various alternatives. Meanwhile, the artist has made an elephantlike design which is not quite achieved.

2] The three creatures hit simultaneously upon "Ev. O. Lution" as their slogan, and they call in the mob to tell them. The mob is a crowd of infrahuman dwarfs, and they file down the center aisle of the audience and salute. The three creatures tell them that the war will soon be over, for evolution is their ally. The mob cheers and leaves.

3] The artist, who has been oblivious to all these goings-on, goes to the curtain of skins at the back of the stage. The three creatures, seeing him for the first time, are aghast. He says he's stuck, and needs another look at the mammoth. They are incredulous, telling him that mammoths are extinct. Hasn't he heard of Civilization, Emancipation, and Progress? Don't kid me, says the artist. It's the Ford's truth! So help me Lenin! they reply. He tears aside the curtain, revealing a steamshovel at work, and crawls out cautiously, as if he were stalking a dangerous animal. The three creatures shrink from the blinding sunlight and close the curtain.

And what is this all about? I think we should notice, in

the first place, that there are two worlds here: the world of routine, which is made up of the politicians and the mob, and the world of transcendent vision, which is made up of the artist and the sunlit world outside the cave. A platonic parable with a difference, this play is Cummings' comment on the nature of reality. The action is built around the solving of two problems—the politicians must find a slogan to pacify the mob, and the artist must get his drawing right—and the meaning of the play emerges from the contrast between these two lines of action and the two worlds they represent.

The point of the solution to the first problem is that it is a complete *non sequitur* and yet that it works anyway. We don't know what they need a slogan for, we don't know why "Ev. O. Lution" is the right one, we don't know what the war is about, and we certainly can infer that whatever it is the slogan will have no real effect upon anything one way or the other. Except that it pacifies the mob; they are pleased and comforted, and they leave cheering. This is a perfect forecast of Madison Avenue's latest motivation research techniques, for the politicians' problem is not so much to win the war as it is to make the mob *think* that the war is being won, just as the huckster's problem is not so much to give the public a product which is actually better than its competitors as it is to make the public *think* that it is better. There is nothing real here at all.

On the other hand, the point of the artist's solution to his problem is simply that he has to go outside and take another look.

But the play as a whole is not quite that schematic, for there are a half-dozen ironies which have still to be accounted for. The basic generating irony is that the politicians, who think and talk as if they were twentieth-century men, actually look and act as if they were cavemen, while the artist, who thinks and talks as if he were a caveman, actually looks and acts like a more advanced creature than they. Now, if we are in the twentieth century, then mammoths *are* extinct and the politicians are right. But their other conceptions belie this one, for their talk of Evolution, Civilization, Emancipation, and Progress is contradicted by their cave, their filthy skins, their fear of the sunlight, the mob of dwarfs and its slavish discipline (remember that their leaders are G, O, and D to them). If we are in pre-history, however, then mammoths are *not* extinct and the artist is right. But the event disproves this, for what is really out there is a steamshovel and not a mammoth.

What are we to make of such anomalies? I think we may draw two related paradoxical morals from these ironies: first, that the twentieth century is in reality morally and aesthetically still pre-historic; and second, that civilized men have become so fixed in their routine categories that they cannot see that a steamshovel can *be* a mammoth. Recall this passage from the Introduction to the 1938 *Collected Poems* (a331):

> . . . If science could fail,a mountain's a mammal. Most-people's wives can spot a genuine delusion of embryonic omnipotence immediately and will accept no substitutes —luckily for us,a mountain is a mammal. The plusorminus movie to end moving,the strictly scientific parlourgame of real unreality,the tyranny conceived in misconception and dedicated to the proposition that every man is a woman and any woman a king,hasn't a wheel to stand on.

The penultimate irony is that the artist, so far as Ev. O. Lution goes, is more advanced than the politicians and their mob, for they are infrahuman while he is a man. Their idea of progress is mechanical—using such oaths as 'the Ford's truth' and 'so help me Lenin' two years before the appearance of Huxley's *Brave New World*—while his is organic. Reality for the artist is not the flat and static surface of categories we learn from civilization to see, but is rather a view beneath the surface where metaphors are born out of Nature's dynamic life. And the final irony is, of course, that what he is drawing is a mechanical product of civilization itself—but for him it is alive, a form to be captured rather than a tool to use. The fact that this play

was written just after the Stock Market Crash is not ac-
cidental, for it was then that the slogans of progress seemed
most hollow. But history has added an irony of its own,
in that we have by now come to learn that Affluence can
be even hollower than Depression—and more dangerous.

ii

In writing *No Title*, Cummings was not content
to talk *about* the rejection of categories, but rather intended to make a book which would *be* a rejection of categories. As he said a decade earlier about one of Lachaise's
pieces: "The Elevation is not a noun, not a 'modern
statue,' not a statue OF Something or Some One BY a
man named Gaston Lachaise—but a complete tactile self-
orchestration, a magnificently conjugating largeness, an
IS" (*Miscellany*, p. 31). If a work of art should be a verb
instead of a noun, then *No Title* is intended to be a verb.

Now there are various ways of achieving organicity, and
the problem here is whether the means chosen are successful. As we have seen, Cummings is still trying to develop
a way of bending language and typography to achieve this
end in his poetry, and he succeeded beautifully in adapting
technique and structure to embody a dynamic interplay of
worlds in *Him*. But what are the means used in *No Title*?
Let's allow Cummings to describe them for us, for
here again he introduces the book with one of his prefatory
imaginary dialogues—a favorite device which betrays an
unhappy knowledge of his audience and a certain amount
of anxiety over that knowledge. You can see he wants to
disabuse the reader's mind of false expectations, and this
is a legitimate aim; but you can also see that he gets more
than a bit defensive at times, thereby alienating the very
audience he seems so anxious to placate. It's clear that he
senses he's in a difficult spot, and wants to be ingratiating
without compromising himself, with the result that he
sometimes winds up in a stance rather more aggressive
than necessary.

This is "An Imaginary Dialogue between ALMOST
Any Publisher And A *certain* Author," and the Publisher

begins: "By all that's holy,THIS IS NOT A BOOK!" It just won't sell, and he continues: "But the damn thing has NO TITLE—the frontispiece is A BLANK—the illustrations DON'T MAKE SENSE—the text is MEANING-LESS—the type suggests a CHILD'S FIRST READER—it's all ABSOLUTELY CRAZY!" This is a pretty accurate description, for the book consists of eight surrealistic tales, averaging around six to eight pages apiece, and each is preceded by a line drawing (with a title and a motto) having no discernible connection with the text. As far as the text is concerned, it's as if Cummings had taken the nonsense from some of Him's speeches three years before and expanded them into a book (at least one, the first chapter, had appeared earlier in different form in 1925—see *Miscellany*, pp. 142–46).

Let me try to outline *No Title* briefly: *Chapter I*. The Garden of Eden . . . *before the dawn of history* . . . The drawing shows an elephant surrounded by other animals, and Adam and Eve cowering in shame. The tale recounts some of the million freakish mishaps which ensued when "The king took off his hat and looked at it" (in the original, they ensued when "Calvin Coolidge laughed"). These are incongruous catastrophes, outrageous disasters, improbable cataclysms. Havoc unmitigated.

Chapter II. The Death of Abraham Lincoln . . . *even prominent people* . . . The drawing shows Lincoln blessing with his large hands a Negro, and another figure with a sword kneeling. The tale begins by telling of Thomas Feeney, master ploughman, Gaga, his wife, and Henry Holt, the village drunk, but soon turns into a surrealistic train ride.

Chapter III. The Swan and Leda . . . *protect your dear ones* . . . The illustration shows what appears to be a goose chasing a little girl who is dropping what appears to be a basket of cookies. I cannot tell what the text is about.

Chapter IV. The Friend in Need . . . *a boon to travellers* . . . The drawing shows a rescue dog named Rover. I cannot say what the text is about.

Chapter V. The Spinster's Dilemma . . . *but a parrot did* . . . The picture shows a woman holding her hands over her ears as her parrot squawks and a man leaves the room. The story deals with the misfortunes of some outlandish dynasty.

Chapter VI. The Helping Hand . . . *nobody is exempt* . . . The illustration shows a man in a rowboat on whose prow are letters which I would guess are a child's version of "POLLY," but I don't see why (it may be a reference to the parrot in the preceding drawing, but that doesn't clarify much). The story is not paraphrasable.

Chapter VII. The First Robin . . . *if the punishment fitted the crime* . . . The illustration shows a prisoner in jail looking prayerfully through his cell window at a robin. The text is obscure.

Chapter VIII. The Dog in the Manger . . . *Aesop knew* . . . The picture shows a horse, a dog, and a laughing man. The tale is about Edna and her daddy on a surrealistic safari.

There is hilarious punning, parodying, and burlesquing going on here, regarding both event and language. These are, in effect, similar to some of those poems which I have been categorizing as comedies. They are extended jokes — and that, I think, is just the trouble. Brevity is the soul of wit, and the point of a joke should be reached quickly and soon dropped. There are limits to the fun of pure nonsense. We recall that the Public, in the imaginary dialogue with the author about *Him*, had said: "So far as I'm concerned, my very dear sir, nonsense isn't everything in life" (*The Magic-Maker*, p. 226). But the nonsense in *Him* almost always had a point, whereas here, if there is a point, I have completely failed to grasp it.

The complaint of the Publisher, then would seem justified. How does the author reply to it? In the *Him* imaginary dialogue, the author had replied by distinguishing among the three voices of life. Here, however, is how the present dialogue continues:

PUBLISHER: . . . —it's all ABSOLUTELY CRAZY!
AUTHOR: I should call it hyperscientific.

PUBLISHER:"HYPERscienTIFic"?

AUTHOR:Why not?The title is inframicroscopic—the frontispiece is extratelescopic—the pictures are superstereoscopic—the meaning is postultraviolet—the format is preautoerogenous.

PUBLISHER:SAY . . . NObody's going to FALL for THAT drivel!

AUTHOR:All the better;everybody'll laugh—

PUBLISHER:"LAUGH"?

AUTHOR:—Heartily.

PUBLISHER:But don't you seem to realize that this stuff is NOT FUNNY:it's JUST MAD!

AUTHOR:Could you speak a little less ambiguously?

PUBLISHER:Listen—I CAN'T UNDERSTAND this RUBBISH which YOU'VE got the INFERNAL NERVE to ask ME to PALM OFF on the UNSUSPECTING PUBLIC as A BOOK: and I'M SUPPOSED TO BE an INTELLIGENT PERSON!

AUTHOR:Is that any reason why you should be afraid to laugh heartily?

PUBLISHER:WHO'S afraid to laugh heartily?

AUTHOR:Certainly not an intelligent person.

PUBLISHER:Oh,so I'M NOT INTELLIGENT—HUH?

AUTHOR:If this book makes you laugh heartily,you are intelligent—

Now here, Cummings had pushed the reader right into that trap he just barely avoided in the Introduction to the 1938 *Collected Poems:* if you don't like the book, then you are stupid. This presumption of success is not calculated to win readers over. The dialogue concludes as follows:

PUBLISHER:And if this BABYISH NONSENSE BORES ME STIFF?

AUTHOR:If this babyish nonsense bores you stiff, you have "civilization"—

PUBLISHER:"CIVILIZATION"?!

AUTHOR:And a very serious disease it is, too—

PUBLISHER:"DISEASE"?

AUTHOR:Invariably characterized by purely infantile delusions—

PUBLISHER:"DELUSIONS"—such as WHICH?

AUTHOR:Such as the negatively fantastic delusion that
something with a title on the outside is a book—
and the positively monstrous delusion that a book
is what anybody can write and nobody can't pub-
lish and somebody won't go to jail for and everybody will understand.

PUBLISHER:Well,if THAT'S not A BOOK,what IS?

AUTHOR:A new way of being alive.

PUBLISHER:(*swallowing his chequebook and dropping
dead*):NO thanks . . .

It is curious that the Publisher should say to the Author
just what Cummings himself was to say five years later to
fourteen hostile publishers. At any rate, what I find difficult here is not the imaginary dialogue or the Author's intentions, for the former is very funny and the latter are
quite intelligible in the light of everything I've been saying
so far about Cummings' writings. Certainly a book is not
a book simply because it looks like one; certainly a book is
a new way of being alive. But the question is: is *this* book
a new way of being alive? It seems to me just as certain
that a book is not a book simply because it *doesn't* look
like one. One does not keep alive simply by avoiding sterile
habits; it is not enough just to step outside the categories,
for one must see more truly once one gets out there. I feel
that we see more truly in *Him*, but I'm afraid I don't see
anything at all in *No Title*.

Unless, of course, laughter is a good in itself. And this is
what Cummings seems to intend. Laughter, which arises
out of incongruity, can indeed be transcendental in thus
breaking down the categories. But when we are taken out
of the categories simply to float surrealistically on a wash of
non sequiturs, then we may indeed fail to transcend. There
is a sense of release, but it is quickly followed by a sense of
frustration as we miss what it is we are being released *for*.
Is it possible that laughter can be as innocent as Cummings implies? That it can have no object, no point?

So we confront once again the paradox of modern or-
ganicism, this time from the other side. By all means, let

us actively engage the reader in the experience of the poem by denying him the props of habit and abstraction, props which tend to become substitutes for the poem itself. So let us frustrate his plot- and logic-expectations, let us bend language to our purpose, let us speak suggestively and symbolically. With this we should have no quarrel; we must, however, judge the fruits of this theory on their own merits, and we can only do so in terms of how well they have succeeded in achieving the end in view. The paradox is that if a work succeeds too well in becoming a verb rather than a noun, it will lose contact with the reader altogether, the very reader whom it anxiously sought to engage. With the best will in the world, many trained readers of modernist literature get very little pleasure out of Pound's *Cantos*, Joyce's *Finnegans Wake*, or Williams' *Paterson*. If we must express no ideas but in things, we may end up expressing nothing at all. No matter how concrete we can force language to become, we should not wring it free of abstractions entirely, for communication depends upon them. We may wish to keep them down to a minimum, and that is a good thing, but we cannot eliminate them without eliminating the reader as well. A true work of art will never be made wholly out of discrete particulars.

Thus, one of the most attractive qualities about *Him* is that it presents such a varied and lively appearance to the audience, while at the same time suggesting meanings and significances. They may keep eluding our grasp, but suggest them it surely does. They are hard to define and paraphrase, which is as it should be, but we know they are there. No such suggestions appear in *No Title* to tease us on, and without them we may (alas!) find ourselves on the side of Cummings' harassed Publisher whose anxiety makes him speak mostly in capitals: "And if this BABYISH NONSENSE BORES ME STIFF?" Maybe this is not a book *about* something, but does that necessarily make it a book?

iii

Tom is a ballet based on *Uncle Tom's Cabin*, and was suggested to Cummings, as the dedication explains, by

Marion Morehouse, the poet's wife. It is written as a combination of synoptic narrative and dance description, but I
shall have to treat it primarily from a literary point of view.
First let us see how Cummings handles the story, and then
go on to compare it with Mrs. Stowe's original, which he
re-read for the purpose.

The ballet is divided into four episodes: *One.* George is
fleeing Haley, a slave trader, who comes to the Shelbys'
plantation. Haley is in possession of the Shelbys' mortgage,
and so forces them to sell Eliza, George's wife, and Tom.

Two. While Eliza tries to escape with her baby over the
ice floes, George is pursued by Haley's slave catchers. As
they are both about to be caught simultaneously, they are
rescued by a group of Quakers.

Three. Meanwhile Haley is bringing Tom by StClare's
New Orleans estate. Eva, StClare's ailing little daughter, is
revived by the sight of Tom, and StClare buys him. Eva
dies, however, and so does her father; his slaves are consequently put up at auction, and Legree, the brutal master
of Cassy, Eliza's mother, buys Tom.

Four. Tom arouses Legree's wrath when they arrive at
the latter's Red River plantation, and Legree beats him to
death. Legree is then extinguished by the spirit of Creative
Nature, who turns into Cassy. George, Eliza, and the child
enter, are reunited with Cassy around Tom's body, and are
surrounded by divine radiance in a final apotheosis, as
Death disappears with Tom's body and the Heavenly Host
appears.

The ballet is preceded by a two-and-a-half page synopsis,
and the text itself takes up almost twenty-seven pages. A
bird's-eye view of the action reveals an artfully balanced
structure:

One:	George-Eliza	Tom
Two:	George-Eliza	
Three:		Tom
Four:	George-Eliza	Tom

The syllogistic symmetry of this pattern is clearly revealed
when we label George-Eliza as A, and Tom as B:

```
        A              B
        A
                       B
        A              B
```

We have, that is, both parts of the story, then one, then the other, and then both again at the end. I believe that this structure suits the stylized manner of its presentation, as well as the formal pattern of separation and reunion, escape and capture, danger and rescue, death and redemption, which organizes the whole. For the plot turns on two redemptions, the first of which serves as the climax of Episode Two, and the second of which serves as the climax of Episode Four, thus reenforcing in another way the structural principle of alternation.

For the theme of the ballet is an allegorical demonstration of how downtrodden Good triumphs over powerful Evil. Cummings' basic conception governing this work is that Good is spiritual while Evil is mere brute force, and thus we can see how he fashions the causes of the action. The first redemption is of the *deus ex machina* sort, in that the Quakers come from nowhere to rescue the helpless fugitives, but their intercession is nevertheless spiritual. Cummings says, in the Synopsis: "Armed only with the Inner Light of personal communion, the Friends of humanity rout its foes" (p. 7). Here is how it reads in the text (pp. 18–19):

> . . .—enter, right- and left-backstage, a group of men and a group of women (the Friends or Quakers) all dressed in gray; all holding bibles over their hearts
>
> outward swooping files of dogmen meet at the middle foreground—crisply advancing grey figures form a single line across the background in front of George and Eliza
>
> inward surges a single file of dogmen—every Friend lowers his or her bible: and all the Quaker hearts glow with an unearthly radiance
>
> —stopped, the column of attackers flattens itself from within outward; darkening, one after one, the dogmasks sink.

The second redemption, however, is truly organic and paradoxical, and is rendered in full transcendental panoply. Whereas Good triumphed over Evil, at the end of Episode Two, by literally defeating it, here Good triumphs over Evil in being defeated *by* it. He who loses his life shall find it, is the moral of this second and final redemption; physical loss is spiritual gain. This is how it's put in the Synopsis: "At the moment of Tom's physical death, murderous perversity is confronted by its opposite, Creative Nature: the white killer cringes before an apparition, symbolizing to his distorted senses the vengeance of the entire black race. As this apparition dissolves in the reality of Cassy, Legree's mentality crumbles; the former prodigy of brute strength becomes a miserable insect, consumed by the merciful radiance of eternal things. . . . Suddenly transcending their personalities, the ecstasy of the three brown protagonists [Cassy, George, and Eliza] overflows. To Judgement trumpets Death enters, black like Tom; and, like Tom's body, Death Itself disappears: appears the Heavenly Host" (9). This is nothing short of a religious miracle, and it is presented as such in the text (pp. 33 ff.) :

> dance of The Eternal Peace . . . Tom(*)
> weightlessly uplifted within textures beneath knowledge,
> an immortal essence swims; floats a serenity completed,
> spiritual, homogeneous, only composing the most giving
> freedom of all joys which are beyond experience.

The chief significance of this work in Cummings' development is that he saw it as a chance to dramatize on the stage an actual moment of self-transcendence. There are at least two reasons why this second redemption is so different from the first: one, that it provides a fitting climax to follow the first; and two, that Tom is a superior being and so is capable of self-transcendence. George and Eliza, rescued by the Quakers, are good enough people, but they are not holy. Tom is portrayed throughout as a patient and god-like man, refusing to flee and refusing to protect himself. He triumphs over Evil by ignoring it, he lives by dying, he conquers through suffering. And it is this which ultimately defeats Evil: Tom neither fears nor resists Evil, and it exhausts itself on him by doing its worst. When the worst is over, the spirit remains. Isn't this what Cummings learned in La Ferté Macé? You are free when you have nothing else to lose.

Those who say that Cummings' treatment of the Negro is condescending have not looked closely at *Tom*, for the black man is not praised for being a contented and obedient servant, knowing his place and accepting his lot in life. That is not why Cummings wants the Negro to remain a Negro. Tom is a spiritual force, and as a child of the Earth, is avenged by her (p. 34):

> dance of Avenging Africa . . . the monstergoddess
>   implacably gliderushing, occultly growpausing, striking
>   like a serpent, dreaming like a forest, one heavenlessly
>   unearthful absence, one kinetically static presence,
>   meaningfully emanates distinct reptilian timelessness,
>   meaninglessly smothers smoking Hell with the illimit-
>   able lushness of impossibility—suddenly blossoming
>   miraculous abstractions, a doomful moultingly vast abso-
>   lute omnipotence points . . . and Nature confronts Sa-
>   tan. . . .

The vital point here is that the principle of Evil is opposed by the principle of Nature, that Evil is not a part of Nature.

Regarding the manner in which this story is presented, a few words may be said. The narrative portions are written as pantomime, while the dance portions are written as formal choreography. In both cases, however, gestures are assigned to symbolize character, and much use is made, as in *Him*, of light, darkness, and space. The language, finally, is equally stylized, making free use of verbal compounds in the effort to describe motion.

Let us see how Cummings' conception compares with that of the original. It goes without saying that, in boiling down a novel of over 500 pages (in the Dolphin paperback edition, Doubleday & Company) into a ballet of less than 27 pages, Cummings had to omit and condense drastically. He took from Mrs. Stowe's book only what he needed from the main line of the action in order to highlight his double escape-pursuit-redemption pattern. To examine his omissions and condensations would be a task too lengthy for the present purpose. What he did retain, however, were the basic lines of characterization regarding the principals: the decency of the Shelbys, the desperation of George, the courage of Eliza, the humanity of StClare, the holiness of Eva and Tom, and the villainy of Legree. But he transformed even what he retained: what he did was to essentialize these traits to suit his allegorical purpose, purifying away the didactic dross of the original.

That is to say, although Mrs. Stowe's conception has a strong spiritual element, her purpose was primarily sociological and humanitarian, while Cummings' is primarily spiritual. Her Christianity, which was basically Protestant and anti-clerical, served as a basis for her humanitarian idealism. What bothered her most of all, as she makes abundantly clear, was that the legalized institution of slavery encouraged the white man to treat the Negro as if he weren't human, as if his familial feelings were non-existent, as if he were insensitive to moral emotions and religious values. Her answer was twofold: to show that, when this *is* the case, it is due to brutal and brutalizing treatment; and that, even under the worst of conditions, some Negroes can retain a humanity which surpasses that of most white men. Having shown the causes of the black man's degradation and the possibility of his redemption, she then goes on to argue for the abolition of the institution itself. And she peppers her pages with little sermons to that effect, often addressing the reader directly in the process.

None of this sociological argument remains, so far as I can see, in Cummings' version. In *Tom* it is not the institution of slavery which is under attack but rather Evil itself. And it is not so much being attacked as it is being defeated: brute power must surrender at last to spiritual force. Mrs. Stowe looks forward to the day of victory, while Cummings shows the day itself. In the original, Tom goes through no apotheosis, and we must wait for earthly means to right his earthly wrongs. In the ballet, the transcendent world achieves one more triumph over the non-world. As he came to see even more clearly eleven years later, in the "Foreword to Krazy," Cummings sees here that love renders hate powerless. Indeed, if we take his vision seriously, we can appreciate the fact that not only did Cummings omit Mrs. Stowe's sociological purpose, he also contradicts it. Not that he would have been against abolition; it's just that he would not have seen it as the cure. In his view, the true solution belongs in another category altogether, a category "whose ways are neither reasoned nor unreasoned" (b, no. 11). For Cummings is, we may recall, a Paradoxer and not a Reformer, and that helps to explain the differences between his ballet and Mrs. Stowe's novel.

ALSO A PERSONAL ACCOUNT, *Eimi* (the title is Greek for "I am") is related to *The Enormous Room* clearly and explicitly—only this time the poet is more than ten years older. The 1932 Introduction to the Modern Library edition of the earlier book points up the connection by means of an author's dialogue with his public (pp. vii–viii):

[Public:] How does Am compare with The Enormous Room?
[Author:] Favorably.
They're not at all similar, are they?
When The Enormous Room was published, some people wanted a war book; they were disappointed. When Eimi was published, some people wanted Another Enormous Room; they were disappointed.
Doesn't The Enormous Room really concern war?
It actually uses war: to explore an inconceivable vastness which is so unbelievably far away that it appears microscopic.
When you wrote this book, you were looking through war at something very big and very far away?
When this book wrote itself, I was observing a negligible portion of something incredibly more distant than any sun; something more unimaginably huge than the most prodigious of all universes—
Namely?
The individual.
Well! And what about Am?
Some people had decided that The Enormous Room

wasn't a just-war book and was a class-war book, when
along came Eimi—aha! said some people; here's another
dirty dig at capitalism.

And they were disappointed.

Sic.

Do you think these disappointed people really hated
capitalism?

I feel these disappointed people unreally hated themselves—

And you really hated Russia.

Russia, I felt, was more deadly than war; when na-
tionalists hate, they hate by merely killing and maiming
human beings; when internationalists hate, they hate by
categorying and pigeonholing human beings.

So both your novels were what people didn't expect.

Eimi is the individual again; a more complex individual,
a more enormous room.

(I am not sure, incidentally, why he implies in 1932 that
Eimi has already been published, when Eimi was published in 1933. Several other anomalies appear in this Modern Library edition: the Introduction is followed by the
author's name, and the notation "New York 1932"; this
Introduction is copyrighted 1934 on the verso of the title
page; and on the recto of the following page is a brief biography and bibliography which gives 1932 as the date
for Eimi.—After having read the manuscript of this book,
however, Mrs. Cummings kindly suggested that perhaps
these puzzles might be solved by the fact that parts of
Eimi were published in The Hound and Horn, spring and
fall, 1932.)

Like The Enormous Room, then, Eimi is a journal or
diary (the term "novel" is used very loosely here) concerning an actual personal experience abroad, and like the earlier book, which was built around archetypal suggestions
from Pilgrim's Progress, Eimi is based lightly on the structure of The Divine Comedy, as embodying a similar archetype of death and rebirth. These lines of resemblance intersect explicitly in two passages in Eimi where Russia as
a kind of Hell reminds him of La Ferté Macé: visiting a
socialist jail, Cummings writes, "Feeling,remembering La

Ferté,now comrade myself descends these steps—treads this unfree earthless" (p. 152); and in getting his exit visa out of Moscow, he says he wants to avoid American tourists, and is queried by an official, "You do not like Americans? (almost can feel myself eyed by La Ferté's commission) / I like people" (p. 233). And like *The Enormous Room*, as its Introduction makes clear, *Eimi* is intentionally apolitical, opposing the living human being to the machinery of the state. To be for or against war, to be for or against capitalism—these would involve Cummings in those very categories he wants to transcend. The real issues are life against death, the individual against society, and not one institution against another. Thus the usual categories cut across the distinctions Cummings wants to make: as an individual can come alive in a prison, so can that prison just as easily be socialist as capitalist. That is why the transcendentalist must so often speak in paradoxes, for his vision runs counter to our ordinary conceptions: where we see life, he sees death; where he sees victory, we see defeat.

The difference, however, between these two books is the difference between youth and maturity. Cummings was twenty-three years old when he was imprisoned in La Ferté, but he was thirty-seven when he visited Russia; twenty-eight when he published *The Enormous Room*, and thirty-nine when he published *Eimi*. Whereas in the first book he was discovering and defining his values, in the second he is applying and confirming them. The structure of *Eimi*, then, involves not so much an upward movement of apocalyptic revelation concerning the Delectable Mountains, as an outward movement of grateful escape as Cummings leaves Russia. The first word of the book is "SHUT" and the last is "OPENS." This experience offered him a chance to test his vision on a large scale, to engage it in a sort of controlled experiment in contrast to mass life. For here was a planned utopia actually coming into being during the violent and depressed thirties, but for Cummings it was simply a more monstrous subhuman superstate than he had been satirizing back home in America. Officialdom was officialdom, he discovered, no matter where it is found—whether in France during the War, in America during the twenties, or Russia during the thirties.

Having discovered himself at last in La Ferté, Cummings now in the Soviet Union is sure he knows what the world is like. And the first discovery is, of course, a necessary condition of the second: the police state is the chief fact of our times, and Cummings stands openly and firmly against it. Even when its goals are benevolent, for in Cummings' mind the end can never justify the means. He will never accept some people telling other people what to do, even when it's for their own good; especially will he not accept *forcing* people to do what is for their own good. In this, he is somewhat similar to Dostoevsky's underground man throwing stones at the Crystal Palace: what is vital to mankind can never be organized into existence. That is why he was as much opposed to the New Deal as he is to Big Business, and critics who say he is inconsistent in castigating the government's efforts to save those same underprivileged classes with whom he sympathizes are, as I have said, completely missing the point. Institutional flaws cannot have institutional remedies, for the defect is built into the machine from the beginning; you cannot undo the damage created by one category by supplanting it with another, but rather must get out of the world of categories altogether. A government must look at men as Man, and therefore no government can save men. Cummings is no more a Republican because he opposes statism than he is a Socialist because he opposes Big Business.

Let us turn now to *Eimi* and see how these conceptions emerge from the experience recorded.

i

It will be useful to begin with an outline so that we may know where we are at any given point. Cummings supplies an outline himself in his "Sketch for a Preface" to the Grove Press edition of 1958 (the text I am using here), but it is rather more detailed and elaborate than the present purpose requires. I have used it to great advantage, however, and what follows is based upon it as well as the book itself.

The journey, which took place in 1931, begins in Paris on May 10, and ends there on June 14. The total time, then, is thirty-six days, or just over five weeks. I divide the book into three parts, with subdivisions, as follows:

I. *Moscow* (twenty-two days).

a) Beginning May 10: two days on train to Moscow. Experiences with fellow passengers, and the red tape of Customs. Twenty days in Moscow.

b) Beginning May 12: eight days with Virgil at Hotel Metropole. Virgil, Cummings' first mentor through Hell, is a fellow-American from the author's home town, Cambridge, Mass. This man is a sympathizer of the Soviet experiment who spends half of each year in Russia studying its theatre. During this period, Cummings comes to know the Hotel and its ways, a Torgsin gift shop, the red tape of a socialist bank and the Intourist office, the presence of the Secret Police, Russian food and trams and street washers and parks and monuments (especially the church of St. Basil); he meets English and American communists, Russian writers, the relatives of friends; and he is taken to parties, shows, and nightclubs.

c) Beginning May 20: twelve days with Turk and Turkess. These gracious people, Jack London's daughter and her husband, invite Cummings to stay with them. The Turkess, so called because her husband is an Assyrian, a wise and gentle man working as a foreign correspondent in Moscow, is also called Beatrice—in relation, of course, to Virgil. Cummings visits a socialist jail during this period, and has problems arranging for his exit visa; he is taken to the Bolshoy Theatre, the Moscow Art Theatre, the Lenin Institute, Lenin's Tomb, and the Museum of Western Art; he meets a nonconforming scientist, a doctor and his family, a socialist family, and Tolstoy's granddaughter; and he goes to the movies and a circus.

II. *Odessa* (eight days).

a) Beginning June 1: two days on train to Odessa via Kiev. Experience with fellow passengers, and red tape.

b) Beginning June 3: six days at Odessa with the Noo Inglundur. This man, also a fellow American, is a travel agent who rescues Cummings from Intourist, thus becoming our pilgrim's third mentor. He assumes control of Cummings' travel arrangements and guides him around town during his stay. They become attached to a "stunned" Italian, an electrical engineer whom the Soviet Union had asked to come and work for Communism but whom it has inexplicably abandoned in Odessa without funds. Cummings is taken to see the Potemkin stairs and the bathing beaches.

III. *Istanbul* (six days).

a) June 9: one day aboard ship to Istanbul. Cummings falls in with a man he calls Dude, and meets other passengers and sailors.

b) Beginning June 10: three days at Istanbul with Roberts College people, and Cummings sees the sights.

c) Beginning June 13: two days by train to Paris.

Although recording the trip chronologically in diary or journal form, *Eimi* is more than a travel book. The events just outlined are conceived of as a journey into and out of Hell, a journey whose nadir is reached just after its midpoint when Cummings visits Lenin's tomb. On May 22 he is taken to a socialist jail, and he recalls Dante's *lasciate ogni speranza* as he enters, and then says: "We all suddenly have entered hell's mouldering pitlike dank well" (p. 151). On May 29 he learns his exit visa has been approved, and he exults: "I'm going,going out of the unworld;now I feel it:now I feel that it's true." And, planning to have his picture taken, he says of the photograph: "Sometime perhaps we'll say to somebody: This is what I wasn't;this is how,without ever dying,I didn't ever live" (p. 226). And on May 30 he goes to Lenin's Tomb, the frozen nadir of the pit wherein dwells Satan himself (p. 241):

Grave.
The grave.
Toward the (grave.

All toward the grave) of himself of herself (all toward the grave of themselves) all toward the grave of Self.

He reflects, upon seeing the famous corpse itself (pp. 243–44):

> Certainly it was not made of flesh. And I have seen so many waxworks which were actual (some ludicrous more horrible most both) so many images whose very unaliveness could liberate Is, invent Being (or what equally disdains life and unlife) — I have seen so very many better gods or stranger, many mightier deeper puppets; everywhere and elsewhere and perhaps in America and (for instance) in Coney Island . . .
>
> now (breathing air, Air, AIR) decide that this how silly unking of Un-, this how trivial idol throned in stink, equals just another little moral lesson. Probably this trivial does not liberate, does not invent, because this silly teaches; because probably this little must not thrill and must not lull and merely must say—
>
> I am Mortal. So Are You. Hello
>
> . . . another futile aspect of "materialistic dialectic" . . . merely again (again false noun, another fake "reality") the strict immeasurable Verb neglected, the illimitable keen Dream denied

And, on June 2, making arrangements for getting from Kiev to Odessa and having the usual red-tape troubles, he comments: "The if nothing else very idiocy of the above-mentioned capitalist comrade Kem-min-kz will somehow actually bring (I feel) him out of hell" (p. 270). From here on in, for the rest of the trip, Cummings refers over a dozen times to his departure from Russia as an escape from Hell (pp. 289, 290, 329, 336, 341, 346–48, 356, 358, 373, 378, 382, 386, 388, 398, 411–12).

ii

And why is the journey imagined and shaped in these terms? I have already indicated the main outlines of an answer—that Russia is a subhuman superstate—but I want now to fill in the details and show just how this experience served as a confirmation of Cummings' transcendental values. There is in his mind a vision of the possibilities of human life, and this he calls the "actual" world; and there is around him the spectacle of a regimented and joyless life, and this he calls the "real" world. Throughout the Moscow portion of the book, these two worlds confront one another, and on rare occasions they intersect and then Cummings reacts with delight to some sign of life which comes unexpectedly into view. But by and large he is oppressed by what he sees—by the people, the city, the food, the officials, the shows, and the general atmosphere. For Russia is a land of Was, which represents, of course, the opposite of Is.

Let us trace first the "real-actual" dichotomy. He says, speaking of Marx (pp. 87–88):

> I marvel that such prophets as KM cannot be poets,that always they must depend upon mere reality,always must attempt a mere realization of themselves by others—
>
> with what fatal consequences!for what could less resemble I wish than It is?less an alive actual tree then the "same" merely not dead tree,"successfully" which has been transplanted?less freedom than unfreedom,less dreaming than doing? . . . yet only the bravest fools have glimpsed that difference;with what eyes! . . .
>
> For the immeasurable domain of The Verb is actually or imagining,which cannot ever be translated(and least of all resembles its reflection in a measurable system of nouns). For life is mercilessly not what anyone believes, and mercifully is life not what a hundred times a thousand times a million anyones believe they believe.

Speaking of the season (May 18), he says: "there is an I feel;an actual universe or alive of which our merely real world or unthinking existence is at best a bad,at worst a murderous,mistranslation;flowers give me this actual universe" (pp. 104–5). He says jokingly later in the day, "a world in the head is worth two unworlds in the hand" (p. 113). Almost a week later he visits a circus, and is overjoyed by its "authentic ripe reek smiting and entire;/the hulking truth of smell," and wonders by contrast how "there should nonexist uncertainly certain gameless games" (pp. 170–71):

each a because or system merely;when fears,wishes-
(placed at certain angles to each other)become facts,boxes.
If the game or system is unkind,these boxes are cages;-
through which even may communicate(peering sometimes)the defined inhabitants. And if the system or because is kind,these boxes have no perforations and these-
(ignorant of ignorance)prisoners do not suspect that they
are these prisoners. And each measurably system(and
miserably)must remain negative,merely must remain
real;must dreamless mean,untruth

e.g. an altruistic game of human prisoners,uncircus of
noncreatures,calling itself "Russia." Almost—now I ap-
prehend—are within whose realness decently embedded
hints(directions,pressures)of actuality

Feeling the dangerous thrill of being in non-Commu-
nist Turkey, toward the end of his journey, he almost sings
(p. 380):

(pity poor realists!
all whose minds cannot wish;
those who do not dare,
have lost their wonder)

Russia, then, is a realist's world, a world without vitality
and imagination, a world of Was (p. 8), of "strictly om-
nipotent whichnessandwhatness," of "such nonlife and
such undeath" (p. 10). "Above,around,unbelievable ema-
nation of ex-;incredible apotheosis of isn't" (p. 15). "Ver-
ily,verily have I entered a new realm,whose inhabitants are
made of each other" (p. 21). Marxism is "a joyless experiment in force and fear" (p. 49). "There are not many
things in Moscow that shine. I'm a child. I like shining
things" (p. 64). He's amazed at the way the street sprin-
klers drench pedestrians, and is told that they "can't be
turned off. That's Russia!" (pp. 106–7):

the actuality of which metaphor gives me pause. I actually feel(at that moment)how perfectly the far famed revolution of revolutions resembles a running amok street-
sprinkler,a normally benevolent mechanism which attains
—thanks(possibly)to some defect in its construction or
(possibly)to the ignorance or(probably)playfulness of its
operator—distinct if spurious loss of unimportance;certain

transient capacity for clumsily mischievous behaviour . . .
very naturally whereupon occur trivial and harmless catastrophes

"Machinemade 'civilization' isolates every human being
from experience(that is,from himself)by teaching mankind to mistake a mere gadgety interpretation(e.g.the
weatherman's prediction)of experience for experience it-
self(e.g.weather)" (p. 142). At one point Cummings ex-
plodes, "That's what's lousy here!Trying!everybody's never
feeling;never for a moment relaxing,laughing,wondering—
everybody's solemnly forever focussing upon some laugh-
less idiotic unwonderful materially nonexistent imperma-
ence,which everybody apparently has been rabotatically
['rabota' means 'work'] instructed tovarich to welcome.
God damn undream! May the handshaking hell of the
Elks and morons bugger to a bloody frazzle everybody who
spends his nonlife trying to isn't" (p. 197). On the Orient
Express, thinking back over his recent visit, he muses to
the tune of the train's moving wheels (parodying Aragon's
poem, *The Red Front*, he's been translating): "USSR a
USSR a night- USSR a nightmare USSR home of the
panacea Negation haven of all(in life's name)Deathwor-
shippers hopper of hate's Becausemachine(U for un- &S
for self S for science and R for -reality)how it shrivels:how
it dwindles" (p. 413).

And what is the world in the mind which is worth two
unworlds in the hand? "Long live Is! Up—in the holy
name of uncommon NonSense! Viva!" (p. 48). And (p.
101):

"tell him I drink . . . to the individual."
A pause "he says that's nonsense."
"Tell him I love nonsense and I drink to nonsense." Pause
"he's very angry. He says you are afraid"
"tell him I am afraid to be afraid"
noisemusic,a waiter's glaring. "He believes you are mad."
    "Tell him:a madman named noone says,that someone
is and anyone isn't;and all the believing universe cannot
transform anyone who isn't into someone who is"

To be alive, to be an individual, is to escape the categories of sense into the transcendent sphere of nonsense. It is to grow, which "is much harder than even being born" (pp. 230–31):

> People may dare to live,people may be taught or may teach themselves death;noone can learn growing. Noone can dare to grow. Growing equals that any reason or motive or unreason becomes every other unreason or reason or motive. Here exists no sign, no path. No distance,and no time. The grower has not any aim,not any illusion or disillusion,no audience. Not even a doubt:for he is doubt;-perfectly all outward or inward points of reference are erased.

And to be alive is to be able to love. Cummings reflects, upon hearing a phonograph playing a love song on board the ship to Istanbul (p. 356):

> Alive is singing of love(what else is there to sing of?)-Voice is climbing toward love(what else is there to climb toward?)& a Song is feels(inventing)being(feels is imagines)-mov ingcrea ting(Only is For and always Is and was And only shall be for always Love!
>
> without whom nothing is everything does not exist; or shadows. Kingdom of hell,Un)

The kingdom of hell is where lovelessness is; hence is Russia a kind of Hell. In this kingdom people inhabit an idea instead of themselves (p. 181), and here the artist is asked to serve the state, and "for someone who believes that art is above everything else,who has oldfashioned ideas like that,who cannot participate in the struggle,who is unable to do anything—it's hard" (p. 68). Cummings sees a play in Moscow and is pleased at the beginning as he senses an authentic work of art unfolding: "For I taste technique:-smell style;touch something(not definably,particularly,logically which seems)thoroughly which Is:understanding the spectator always a never faster than the spectator overstands it." But then something happens to spoil it: "Dogma—the destroyer of happens,the killer of occurs,the ugliness of premeditatedly—here stalks And How" (p. 58). And propaganda takes over.

For the artist works by intuition and not ideas, the individual human being and not humanity (p. 137). A lady from Cambridge accuses him of being just like a little boy, and he accepts it as a compliment, saying "that,being a child(and not ashamed)I actually feel these people(actually who are children)directly,entirely;and not as per theories." Then he says, shocking her further, "down with thinking. Vive feeling!" (p. 212):

> bitterly "the world needs thinking!" her unself insists
> "are you the world?"
> defiantly "I'm a part of it!" and contemptuous "—but you're really not!"
> "quite so. Actually,the world is a part of me. And—I'll egocentrically tell the world—a very small part"

The world here, of course, is the world of routine and abstraction. For what Cummings opposes to this world is that of the transcendent vision (pp. 187–88):

> We of whom Is partakes,only to whom our deaths are births—savagely makers beneath docile time(and beyond conquerable space travellers)who are not contained or comprised,who cannot fail in wonder. . . .
> continue not to be,arithmetic of unwish!die on,measure with your nonexistence our existings. . . .
> & live—lovers of To Be!eyes of the world,relax;open and feel,give yourselves only to the giving walls of this single house—only whose ceilings and whose floors frame the Self's full perfect doom of imperfection.

Not that there are not moments of such vision in Russia, for Cummings experiences several such moments himself—on seeing the stars at night (p. 265, cf. p. 377) and a spring rain (pp. 305–6), and even upon experiencing the generosity of some fellow passengers on a train (p. 315). There are beautiful things and some real human beings in Russia (pp. 63, 169, 290, 335), but as for the rest: "What are skies and trees to you?and moons worlds smells stars suns flowers?they are nothing(and Love,what is Love to you?nothing!you create nothing;therefore you cannot

Love,and because you cannot Love you create nothing)—" (pp. 402–3).

But (pp. 116–17):

> something's certain:Eros wins. Eros wins;always:through
> a million or a trillion million selves,musically which are I
> who always cannot perish—plural:the nonworld of
> denial;spectres of defeat,repression;shadows of agony—
> singular:form of all names;ecstacy,triumph,immeasurable
> yes and beautiful explosion . . .
>
> therefore;he(whatever his creed)who would subvert
> Eros,the form,shall become shadow. Who would any
> when or where limit(however hugely)miserably must un-
> die the least undeath of measures;always cannot always
> live;believingly may therefore trivially multiply or worship
> the mere nonexistence of himself.

The climactic moment of transcendence comes toward
the end of the book when Cummings, in the Balkans en-
route to Paris, taking advantage of the train's having
stopped, walks up to the engine and utters the following
prayer (pp. 418–19):

> metal steed,very treacherously wherefrom descending the
> promiscuous urbans plundered rus!through you I greet all
> itgods. And I tell them of a singular He,indivisable[sic]
> or individual,one Being natural or unafraid,for whom exists
> no sign no path no distance and no time. Strutcringing
> inexistence!through you I greet all cruelly enslaving deities
> of perfection. And I tell them of a totally adventuring Is
> who breathes,not hope and not despair,but timeless deep
> unspace—I prophecy to handless them that they shall fall
> by His hand,even by the hand of Poietes;for guilt may not
> cancel instinct and logic defeat wish,nor shall tasteless hate
> obtain against the fragrance of amazement.

And he concludes with the Taoist beatitudes:

> he who knoweth the eternal is comprehensive;
> comprehensive,therefore just;
> just,therefore a king;
> a king,therefore celestial;
> celestial,therefore in Tao;
> in Tao,therefore enduring;
> without hurt he suffereth the loss of the body

When Matthew Arnold appealed, in "Dover Beach," to personal love as the only bulwark against the armies of chaos, he was consciously settling for second best. Clearly, love between man and woman was a poor substitute for the unified faith of bygone days. But those who criticize Cummings either for opposing the Soviet Union with so puny a weapon as love, or for proposing to solve the problems of society so naïvely, ought not to confuse what he means by love with the sort of thing Arnold has in mind. For Cummings, love is precisely that unified faith which Arnold saw it as a substitute for. The more I study *Eimi*, the more I am impressed by its richness of vision. This is no record of visits to factories, collective farms, folk-festivals, political meetings, and the like, for Cummings shows no interest at all in the economic organization of Russia. What he is interested in is the way people live and react to life, and who is to deny that he saw things truly? Is it not becoming tragically clearer each year that the conflict between the United States and the Soviet Union is not so much a conflict between freedom and slavery as it is between one kind of mass society trying to outvie the other? *Eimi* does not deserve the neglect it has received, for it is one of the major documents of our time.

iii

The real problem, of course, is the obscurity of its style. Since the focus is not on *what* happens, but rather on *how* it appears to the traveller, the book gives the appearance of a lack of selectivity, of an impressionistic completeness and fulness. The style is therefore full of nonsyntactical detail, with few transitions or explanations. The reader has to find his way as best he can through what amounts to a notation technique which strives to keep as close as language will allow to the original experience. Cummings said, on this score (Norman, p. 286):

1— that *Eimi's* source equals on-the-spot-scribbled hieroglyphics

2— that, through my subsequent deciphering of said hieroglyphics, not one incident has been revalued; not one situation has been contracted or expanded; not one significance has been warped; not one item has been omitted or inserted.

"Pour l'artiste, voir c'est concevoir, et concevoir, c'est composer" (Paul Cézanne).

The function of this style is not only to reproduce the sense of immediacy, as this was analyzed in connection with the style of *The Enormous Room*, to capture and retain the flavor of the journal or diary as source, but also to enable Cummings to keep his identity in a subhuman superstate. He does so by remaining himself, and by remaining himself he triumphs. On the train to Moscow at the beginning he meets a former White Russian officer who, upon learning that the poet's "visit is quite negligibly pacific," says, " 'why I think they ought to be more afraid of you than of me'(chuckling horribly)'—I'm all through with 'em;but writing's . . . dangerous' " (p. 4).

The language rests upon the extensive and systematic use of two prefixes and a suffix: "non-," "un-," and "-less." By these means Cummings renders the sense of negation which he feels is at the heart of socialist life, and he does so by keeping at the same time the word whose opposite this negation represents, thereby reminding us just what it is that has been denied. Thus, the people of mass society are "unyous" (p. 402), that is, people who are not "you's," people to whom the personal pronoun cannot be applied. Or more complexly, he gets an irony of negation, as when a woman is called a "nonman," that is, masculine without being male. Or, climactically, the prefix or suffix may be used alone, as in "all false timid all -Less all Un-" (p. 402).

We recall Cummings' initial reaction to what promised to be a good play: "I taste technique:smell style:-touch something(not definably,particularly,logically which seems)thoroughly which Is:understanding the spectator always a never faster than the spectator overstands it" (p. 58). It seems to me that the style of *Eimi* pays off, once we give over our anxiety to be sure of each literal detail and focus on the real heart of the matter—the writer's impressions. And these are not negligible, for they are organized by a profoundly mystical sensibility. If we can do this, then the book becomes not only easy to read but also a genuine artistic delight. It takes hold of us and floods us with the immediacy of vision which it is the artists' purpose to ensnare. As the author said in the playbill written for *Him*, the work should understand us rather than be understood by us. If we are not afraid, that is, to surrender ourselves to it.

CUMMINGS' FIRST BOOK of the forties contains, of course, 50 poems, and they are numbered consecutively without further divisions. They may, however, be grouped for comparative purposes in a fashion roughly similar to that already used for the preceding volumes of poetry:

1] Satires, Jokes, and Social Comment—contains eleven poems, which represents a fairly constant proportion so far of this kind of poem in relation to the volume as a whole. And, as might be expected, these poems reflect the social and political conditions of the late thirties: poverty, the rise of certain leftist poets in England, the loss of the art-for-art's-sake ideal, the menace of totalitarianism, a pseudointellectual statesman, the failure of democracy as a political ideal, mostpeople, commercialism, the rise of Stalin and Hitler, and so on (3, 6, 8, 11, 13, 14, 24, 25, 28, 39, 40).

Some of these poems are devoted simply to locating and defining the bad and, by means of puns and parody, denouncing it (a357–58, no. 11*):

> red-rag and pink-flag
> blackshirt and brown
> strut-mince and stink-brag
> have all come to town
>
> some like it shot
> and some like it hung

* Copyright, 1940, by E. E. Cummings and reprinted by permission of Harcourt, Brace & World, Inc.

> *and some like it in the twot*
> *nine months young*

Parades and uniforms, says this latter-day nursery rhyme, simply add up to cannon fodder. Something similar is done by means of the viciously ironic and punning obscenities of "the way to hump a cow is not" (a359–60, no. 14), which retails some good advice on how to get oneself elected by fooling the electorate: not by screwing them outright, but rather by drawing "a line around the spot/ and [calling] it beautifool":

> *the way to hump a cow is not*
> *to push and then to pull*
> *but practicing the art of swot*
> *to preach the golden rule*

Others, however, carry on Cummings' own private meteoric burlesk melodrama by setting up an opposition between the bad and the good. In "these people socalled were not given hearts" (a366, no. 24), for example, he spends eleven lines dissecting the lifelessness of mostpeople, and concludes in the last three lines of the sonnet by opposing to them "the only mystery of love." Likewise, in "as freedom is a breakfastfood" (a366–67, no. 25), he spends three seven-line stanzas in saying that as long as real values are inverted, things will continue to go badly:

> *as hatracks into peachtrees grow*
> *or hopes dance best on bald men's hair* . . .
> *—long enough and just so long*
> *will the impure think all things pure*
> *and hornets wail by children stung*

But then in the fourth and final stanza he reverses his field and concludes on a note of love:

> *worms are the words but joy's the voice*
> *down shall go which and up come who*
> *breasts will be breasts thighs will be thighs*
> *deeds cannot dream what dreams can do*
> *—time is a tree(this life one leaf)*
> *but love is the sky and i am for you*
> *just so long and long enough*

The relationship, then, between the bad and the good in Cummings' world should be clear: the bad is the reverse of the good, and the bad is that which is denounced in the purely invective poems, while the good is that which is celebrated in the love and transcendental poems, so that they are opposed either explicitly or implicitly throughout. If in the world of routine "robins never welcome spring," just so in the natural and transcendent world they always do.

2] The City—contains one poem, which represents a marked decrease in subjects drawn from the streets, the bars, and the brothels. In fact, such an interest, which was so strong in the early volumes, dwindles to practically nothing in the later ones. The poem in question, "spoke joe to jack" (a357, no. 10), portrays what appears to be a barroom brawl over a girl.

3] Impressions—contains five poems, which also represents something of a falling off. Is it possible that there is a kind of tie-in between these diminishings and the increase of interest, which we will discuss in a moment, in such subjects as love and people—that a turning from description and the demimonde involves a turning toward praise and love? As we shall see, the proportions shift once again in the fifties, with love and people decreasing and impressions increasing. At any rate, these poems portray a bare autumn scene, a sea-moon-street scene, a twilight scene, the emergence of a star, and a bird in a tree (1, 7, 32, 44, 47). Cummings' concern with spring and fall, twilight and star-rise, moon and bird, it should be evident, is governed by his fascination with process, movement, and nature's dynamic moments. For these are dynamic images, and his portrayals of them represent the varieties of transition.

4] Love and Transcendence—contains twelve poems, which represents a rise. Although *No Thanks* and *New Poems*, as we have seen, contain a goodly proportion of transcendental poems, they tended not to be explicitly associated with the lover and his lady, and I found only two poems out of ninety-three which were actually love poems.

In *50 Poems*, however, the transcendental attitudes all seem now to be so associated, and the love poems occupy almost a quarter of the book (5, 18, 26, 27, 29, 38, 41, 42, 43, 45, 49, 50). In "am was. are leaves few this. is these a or" (a354, no. 5), for example, a dead fall scene is described, and the concluding lines say:

> We're
>> alive and shall be:cities may overflow(am
>> was)assassinating whole grassblades,five
>> ideas can swallow a man;three words im
>> -prison a woman for all her now:but we've
>> such freedom such intense digestion so
>> much greenness only dying makes us grow

The "dying" refers, of course, to the surrender of the routine world and the abstract categories it imposes upon the natural world, for fall is as much a part of the cycle of growth to the transcendentalist as is spring. And here emerges Cummings' mature paradoxical vision fully developed: compare "for love beginning means return" (a378, no. 38), "love is more thicker than forget" (a381, no. 42), and "enters give whose lost is his found" (a382, no. 45).

My favorite in this group is a beautifully articulated love-sonnet (a381, no. 43 *):

> hate blows a bubble of despair into
> hugeness world system universe and bang
> —fear buries a tomorrow under woe
> and up comes yesterday most green and young
>
> pleasure and pain are merely surfaces
> (one itself showing,itself hiding one)
> life's only and true value neither is
> love makes the little thickness of the coin
>
> comes here a man would have from madame death
> neverless now and without winter spring?
> she'll spin that spirit her own fingers with
> and give him nothing(if he should not sing)

---

* Copyright, 1940, by E. E. Cummings and reprinted by permission of Harcourt, Brace & World, Inc.

how much more than enough for both of us
darling. And if i sing you are my voice,

Hate creates a world of despair, and when this bubble ex-
plodes, the resultant fear dreads the future and hugs the
past. Hate, of course, is the opposite of love, which is giving; hate, then, is taking, and taking is self-defeating for,
since it wants, it can always lose. This possiblity of losing
creates a despair which colors the world, but when reality
breaks through the hater can only fear the natural world
of mutability and he tries desperately to hang on to what
he has in the face of the oncoming future. But pleasure (in
holding on to things) and pain (in losing them) are not
real values, for these are the consequences of taking; giving, or love, is the actual substance of life, the thickness of
the coin showing pleasure on one side and pain on the
other. Would a man ask a reprieve from death, wanting
the false eternity of a static nature (cf. Wallace Stevens'
"Sunday Morning")? Death will flip the coin of his spirit
—a coin with only face-value—and heads she'll win, tails
he'll lose. She will give him nothing, no reprieve—especially if he makes no songs out of his demands. Then the
poet says, speaking as the lover to his lady, that nothing is
more than enough for both of us, for we have asked for
no reprieve in the first place. Out of this, he concludes, he
will make a song, except that he will use her voice in doing
so, she being the subject of his song.

5] People—contains sixteen poems, which represents
the largest single group, a little less than a third of the
book. This interest seems to have emerged in the mid-
thirties, and it reaches its peak here, although it does
continue in the succeeding volumes. He speaks of tramps
waiting for nothing, of an ugly man nobody loves, a tatter-
demalion, a couple who live across the way, a girl sleeping, the strange people of a certain town, an old lady, three
couples dancing in a room, two nuns walking in the spring,
maids and men, some admired friends, a negro playing
the guitar, his (the poet's) father, a Jewish tailor, and some
trapeze artists (2, 4, 9, 15, 17, 19, 20, 21, 22, 23, 31, 33, 34,

35, 36, 48). It seems to me that Cummings' interest in people—and especially those who are strangers in society or who are creative in some special way—has not been sufficiently remarked. He does, of course, have all the usual concerns of the lyric poet: himself, his likes and dislikes, nature, the seasons, love, and so on. But this group of poems adds a special dimension to the work of a man who is often regarded as merely a minor lyricist, and a snob at that.

There remain five poems which I have found unclassifiable or obscure (12, 16, 30, 37, 46).

Technically and stylistically, 50 *Poems* marks several advances. Although there seems to be less concern with radical typographical experiments in the forties than in the thirties, there are other devices being developed. The use of the visual stanza, for example, is becoming more complex and more controlled. Instead of simply setting up his free verse lines in groups of four, Cummings is arranging them in various alternating patterns. The first three poems, for instance, contain visual stanzas built on the following designs: 4–1–4–1–4–1–4–1,   1–3–1–3–1–3–1–3–1–3–1–3–1, 1–2–2–1–2–2–1–2–2–1. There are, however, correspondingly more regularly rhymed and metered quatrains among the conventional stanzas.

Two other developments require comment. The first is what appears to be a new sense of the possibilities of syntactical dislocation. Let us look at the opening lines of a sonnet already discussed in another connection (a354, no. 5):

> am was.   are leaves few this.   is these a or
> scratchily over which of earth dragged once
> -ful leaf.

In combination with elements drawn from his conceptual vocabulary, Cummings is here arranging words discontinuously in much the same fashion that the pointillist arranges colors. And for much the same reason: so that they will be blended by the eye, or in this case, the mind's-eye. Let me risk a paraphrase for the sake of analysis. I think "am was" means that life is gone—it is autumn. Then grammatical number as well as tense blends in "are few leaves this. is these." There are, in other words, a few leaves left on the trees, but they are so few that the poet hesitates to say either "these are" or "this is," so he says in effect "this are" and "these is." As for the rest—"or"— what were once leaves are dragged scratchily over a which (a thing, not alive) of earth. Thus does the atomistic syntax attempt to reduplicate verbally the dry rustling deadness of the scene.

The uses of this device are not confined to scenic description, for he uses it in no. 10 to capture the confusion of a brawl, in no. 16 to create transcendental intensity, and in no. 43 to gain the effect of musical balance.

Which brings us to the second new development: a fresh exploitation of the musical values of balanced and incremental phrasing. There are many poems in this volume which use a refrain, and there are even more which build up a system of phrasal symmetry to create what amounts to a song-form on the page. Look, for example, at "Six/ are in a room's dark around" (21), "a pretty a day" (23), "buy me an ounce and i'll sell you a pound" (27), "anyone lived in a pretty how town" (29), "these children singing in stone a" (37), "up into the silence the green" (41), "love is more thicker than forget" (42), "(sitting in a tree-)" (47), or "i am so glad and very" (49). What we have in most of these poems is that effect of going around again through the same melody with different words which one gets when he sings a song with two or more verses. This is the opposite of that effect of violence and dislocation which Cummings strives for in many satires and certain descriptions by disrupting the typography; this is an effect, by and large, of entranced harmony and unity. Hence it is used most often, as would be supposed, in poems of pleasure, joy, love, fulfilment, and transcendence.

Let us look more closely at a representative example, which, as it happens, has actually been twice set to music (a381, no. 42 *):

> love is more thicker than forget
> more thinner than recall
> more seldom than a wave is wet
> more frequent than to fail
>
> it is most mad and moonly
> and less it shall unbe
> than all the sea which only
> is deeper than the sea
>
> love is less always than to win
> less never than alive
> less bigger than the least begin
> less littler than forgive
>
> it is most sane and sunly
> and more it cannot die
> than all the sky which only
> is higher than the sky

The symmetry is built most obviously by the use of rhyme and meter to create four quatrains, the first and third of which are composed of alternating tetrameter and trimeter lines, and the second and fourth of which are composed entirely of trimeter lines. The next device which comes into view is the corresponding alternation in phrasing: the first stanza is built on the "love is more" phrase, and the third is built on the "love is less" phrase, while the second and fourth are built on the "it is most" phrase. And as one looks more carefully at the poem in these terms, he begins to see how almost every word falls into place according to this design: how "forget" balances "recall," the "sea" balances the "sky," "most mad and moonly" balances "most sane and sunly," and so on. And what is being said here, of course, is all part of the same tune, for these parallels are working in part to create a set of apparent resemblances which turn out on close inspection to be contradictions. And the contradictions are working to build the paradox which is at the heart of the poem, that love is transcendent and ineffable, yet real and tangible. One would think of "forget" as "thin," for example, and not as "thick," for forgetting implies a fading away, a loosening, a disappearing. Thus, to say that "love is more thicker than forget," with the help of an ungrammatically emphatic double comparative, is to say that love is more substantial than a fading memory. But, on the other hand, it is "more thinner than recall," which means it isn't quite as "thick" as remembering either. In other words, love exists tenuously somewhere between forgetting and remembering. What the music accomplishes here, then, is to wind up the metronome of these paradoxes and set them dancing. And this effect, it seems to me, is the special feature of *50 Poems*, one of the chief clues to its significance in the story of Cummings' development.

ii

Four years later Cummings published another fifty-four poems under the title 1 × 1 [One Times One], his second mathematical title, signifying the unity and wholeness of the transcendental vision. The poems here are numbered consecutively, but they are also divided into three groups which match each of the three elements in the title: "1" contains sixteen poems (I–XVI), "×" contains twenty-four poems (XVII–XL), and the second "1" contains fourteen poems (XLI–LIV). There seems to be a loose principle of division at work here, for the first group contains mostly satirical poems, the third contains mostly affirmative poems, while the second contains both kinds. I think the picture will be clearer, however, if we arrange and discuss them according to the slightly stricter system already used above:

1] Satires — contains thirteen poems, which represents a fairly constant proportion. And here, of course, are reflected the events of the early years of the forties, for Cummings has sharp things to say about the arrogance of the Anglo-Saxon condescending to his Oriental enemy, the sale of United States scrap iron to Japan, and the development of science (VII, XIII, XIV), as well as about mass society and various of its people, politicians, salesmen, anthologists, advertizing, alarmists, and man's irritable

reaching after fact and reason (IV, V, VI, VIII, IX, X, XI,
XII, XV, XXVI). For example (a404, no. XXVI *):

> *when god decided to invent*
> *everything he took one*
> *breath bigger than a circustent*
> *and everything began*
>
> *when man determined to destroy*
> *himself he picked the was*
> *of shall and finding only why*
> *smashed it into because*

The last three lines rely rather heavily on Cummings' conceptual vocabulary, and so may call for paraphrase, although they say exactly what they mean once the reader
adjusts himself to verbs, adverbs, and conjunctions being
used as nouns. The "was of shall" means, it seems to me,
the dead fact as opposed to the living possibility, the past
rather than the future, the fixed *versus* the growing. Having settled for this, man searched into its causes, and finding only mysteries, reduced them to knowledge. But Cummings recommends, we recall, that we look for "the beautiful answer who asks a more beautiful question" (a332).

2] Impressions—contains five poems, which, as was already pointed out, represents a falling off. They include
the emblematic opening description of an autumn scene,
a twilight scene, a slip of a moon, a flower, and a sunrise
(I, XVII, XXXI, XLI, XLII). Although typographical
experimentation drops to a new low in this volume, two of
the half dozen or so poems which notably disrupt the page
belong to this group (XXXI and XLI). The first begins
(a407):

> *a-*
>
> *float on some*
> *?*
> *i call twilight you*

and the second (a414):

> *how*
>
> *tinily*
> *of*
>
> *squir(two be*
> *tween sto*
> *nes)ming a gr . . .*

And the function of these disarrangements is to capture the feel of a visual impression.

3] Love and Transcendence—contains twenty-eight poems, which represents a continuing increase, for these poems occupy just over half of the volume as a whole, most of them appearing in the second and third divisions of the book. Two, however, are found in the first section: the poem about going over the wall to eat the forbidden apple (III), and "one's not half two. It's two are halves of one" (XVI). The former is a kind of revision of the paradise myth in which salvation rather than damnation results from the theft, for the command has been given not by God but by society (a390):

> *then over our thief goes*
> *(you go and i)*
> *has pulled(for he's we)*
> *such fruit from what bough*
> *that someone called they*
> *made him pay with his now.*

Cummings frequently constructs a moral balance by using the personal pronouns—i, you, we, they—in this way. "i" plus "you" equals "we," and this is opposed to "they." Often, "we" refers to the lovers, sometimes to the speaker and the reader, and sometimes ambiguously to either or both. In this case, I cannot decide, although I think it refers to speaker and reader as in the Introduction to *New Poems:* "The poems to come are for you and for me and are not for mostpeople— . . . . You and I are human beings;mostpeople are snobs" (a331). At any rate, it is no true divinity who forbids us to eat of the fruit, and therefore the fruit represents not the knowledge of good and evil but transcendental insight into natural process:

> Each why of a leaf says
> (floating each how)
> you're which as to die
> (each green of a new)
> you're who as to grow
> but you're he as to do

The latter poem, a sonnet addressed apparently to the lady, asserts by means of mathematical metaphors the mystical unity of the intuitive vision, of which love is a chief part. The world of unity is a world of quality as opposed to categories of quantity, for the world of quantity is a world of number and hence of multiplicity rather than unity. The world of quality transcends number, "than/ all numerable mosts the actual more." The categories of quantity compromise, of course, the world of knowledge as opposed to that of wisdom:

> —beware of heartless them
> (given the scalpel,they dissect a kiss;
> or,sold the reason,they undream a dream)

And the speaker concludes by re-affirming once again the mystic paradox he has recently begun to grasp: "All lose, whole find" (a398).

Sixteen poems dealing with love and transcendence are found in the second section. Number XVIII shows the speaker making the transition from one world to the next, and concludes: "(really unreal world,will you perhaps do/ the breathing for me while i am away?)" (a399–400); XIX is a praise of the lady's transcendental effect upon the speaker; XX is the well-known "what if a much of a which of a wind," containing another paradoxical affirmation at its conclusion—"the most who die,the more we live" (a401); XXI contrasts the state unfavorably with the individual; XXII defines a poet; XXIII defines love and lovers; XXIX advises the lady to give up the ordinary world in favor of love; XXXII is a love poem; XXXIII praises the lady's eyes and breasts; XXXIV is a definition of love; XXXV praises the lady; XXXVI speaks of true lovers; XXXVII assures the lady of the speaker's love; XXXVIII speaks of affirmation as opposed to doubt; XXXIX tells of the timeless world of lovers; and XL shows the speaker praising the lady for her effect upon him.

I would like to discuss XXXIX a bit further (a412 *):

> all ignorance toboggans into know
> and trudges up to ignorance again:
> but winter's not forever,even snow
> melts;and if spring should spoil the game, what then?
>
> all history's a winter sport or three:
> but were it five,i'd still insist that all
> history is too small for even me;
> for me and you,exceedingly too small.
>
> Swoop(shrill collective myth)into thy grave
> merely to toil the scale to shrillerness
> per every madge and mable dick and dave
> —tomorrow is our permanent address
>
> and there they'll scarcely find us(if they do,
> we'll move away still further:into now

This is a brilliantly constructed poem about the world of knowledge and time as opposed to the world of intuition and timelessness, and a goodly bit of mileage is gotten out of the central metaphor of the toboggan-slide. We have just read in the preceding poem that "yes is a pleasant country:/ if's wintry" (a412, no. XXXVIII), and here we see that winter is the season of the intellect: the ground is covered and the seeds lie frozen within, so that the mind in its quest for certainty slides up and down over the surface without over penetrating beneath. Furthermore, its quest is self-defeating, for as it slides down into knowledge it only has to trudge back up to ignorance again in order to start over. Ignorance, that is, represents the peak, for here the mind is open, while knowledge the nadir, for here the

* Copyright, 1944, by E. E. Cummings and reprinted by permission of Harcourt, Brace & World, Inc.

mind is closed, and it must go up to go down, finally ending up nowhere. But when reality breaks through this sterile game with the melting of the snow and the coming of spring, it becomes impossible to keep sliding up and down over the surface. Well then, says the speaker, history consists of winter sports like this—the world of time is the world of the intellect and unreality—and it just doesn't contain enough of these sports to satisfy his needs, much less his and his lady's needs. Keep on sliding down into knowledge, therefore, he says to this "shrill collective myth," only to scale the slopes back up to ignorance, for he and his lady live in a totally different world and hence are beyond the clutches of history. They live in a timeless world whose permanent address is tomorrow; that is, a world of infinite potentiality, as opposed to the limited historical world of the past. But, and here the poem redoubles its effect remarkably, even more transcendent is the world of the present moment which has neither memory nor hope and is therefore truly timeless: if the future is not far enough away from history, then "we'll move away still further" into the present. Here there'll never find us.

Ten love-and-transcendence poems are found in the third section of the book. Number XLIII identifies love and spring; XLVI asks the reader to open his heart to the poet and receive the treasure of the imaginative vision; XLVII gives the credit to a bird and his song for teaching the poet how to sing; XLVIII praises the lady's eyes; XLIX is another spring and love song; L praises the lady; LI is a third spring and love song; LII is another sonnet of mathematical transcedence; LIII is the lovely kite-flying poem; and LIV is the concluding title-poem celebrating the mystical oneness of love. The development of the song-form, which began to emerge in the preceding volume, continues effectively in 1 x 1, for it contains a half-dozen or more poems built upon the phrasal-balance-and-refrain system which tends to create an affirmative and singing tone. Two appear in the second section (XX, XXIX), and five are to be found in this last section (XLVII, XLIX, L, LI, LIV). Along with this continuing development is found in this book a greater proportion of regular stanza-patterns, apart from the persistent occurrence of sonnets, in relation to the use of the free-verse stanza and typographical distortions. Almost half the poems are written in regular rhyme and meter, and more than one quarter are sonnets. All of which reinforces the impression one gets that 1 × 1 is a distinctively crystallized book, both in art and in vision—a highly-wrought and mature achievement.

THIS SHORT PLAY, which is subtitled "A Morality," was first published in the spring 1946 issue of *The Harvard Wake*, which was devoted to work by and on Cummings. The play came out in book form in December of the same year. I do not have the book edition, nor have I compared it with the magazine version, but on the assumption that there are no significant differences, I shall use the latter as my text.

Santa Claus is divided into five scenes: *Scene One:* The two actors playing the central roles are wearing costumes appropriate to each. Death "wears black tights on which the bones of his skeleton are vividly suggested by daubs of white paint; and his mask imitates crudely the face of a fleshless human skull." Santa Claus is "a prodigiously paunchy figure in faded red motheaten Santa Claus costume, with the familiar Santa Claus mask-face of a be-whiskered jolly old man." It is necessary to establish these details, for, as we shall see, they are involved in the turning points of the action.

Death is strolling, and Santa enters despondently. He is sick at heart, for he has "so much to give; and nobody will take." Although we don't know why he's so despondent at this point, we do learn later that for some reason he has become separated from his wife and child. Death, who is a sharp and witty character, replies that *his* problem is just the opposite, for he has "so much to take; and nobody will give." He offers to help Santa, and begins by explaining why nobody will take what Santa has to offer: people won't take it because they can't. Santa is incredulous: "But surely nothing could be simpler/ than taking something which is freely offered?" Death replies:

> *You're speaking of a true or actual world.*
> *Imagine, if you can, a world so blurred*
> *that its inhabitants are one another*
> *—an idiotic monster of negation:*
> *so timid, it would rather starve itself*
> *eternally than run the risk of choking;*
> *so greedy, nothing satisfies its hunger*
> *but always huger quantities of nothing—*
> *a world so lazy that it cannot dream;*
> *so blind, it worships its own ugliness:*
> *a world so false, so trivial, so unso,*
> *phantoms are solid by comparison.*
> *But no—you can't imagine such a world.*

Santa reflects: "Any more than such a world could imagine me."

Death then explains that what Santa has to give is understanding, the only gift, the only thing which can't be sold. Since the easiest thing to sell is knowledge, he advises Santa to become a Scientist, or, in other words, a knowledge-salesman. When Santa protests that he has no knowledge, only understanding, Death tells him that "the less something exists, the more people want it." Meanwhile, he exchanges his mask and Santa's: underneath his mask is a fleshless human skull, but underneath Santa's is the face of a young man. Santa can't think of something to sell which doesn't exist, so Death suggests a wheelmine. The next scene shows Santa selling wheelmine stock to a crowd of people.

Before going on, however, I feel several things in this first scene require comment. In the first place, we must realize—as is made explicit in the third scene—that Santa doesn't recognize Death. Death acts the part of a helpful friend, and Santa accepts him as such. Similarly, we can't help but accept most of what Death says about the world of mostpeople, for he sounds just like Cummings himself in speaking of that "idiotic monster of negation." Thus a curious paradox is developing: Santa, who has understanding but no knowledge, is naïve about the things of this world and is easily duped by Death; whereas Death, who appears to have understanding as well as knowledge, turns out ultimately, as we have every right to expect, to be the villain. I think the explanation is that Santa is a Reformer who has to learn better, and that Death has true insight but that it is diabolic, for he wants to destroy Santa. After giving Santa an accurate diagnosis of the problem, he deliberately (I think) gives him false counsel, knowing that Santa's becoming a Scientist can only end in disaster.

Scene Two. But Santa is taken in, and we see him here, masked as Death, rather skillfully haranguing a Mob, using, as Reformers sometimes do with the best of intentions, bad means for good ends. And he seems actually to believe in his role, for he tells the Mob that science will free them from their obscene humanity and make them all supermen:

> *Remember: Science*
> *is no mere individual. Individuals*
> *are, after all, nothing but human beings;*
> *and human beings are corruptible:*
> *for (as you doubtless know) to err is human.*
> *Think—only think! for untold centuries*
> *this earth was overrun by human beings!*
> *Think: it was not so many years ago*
> *that individuals could be found among us!*

The irony is clear, for he is promising to turn them into what they already are, as Death has so brilliantly described them, "a world so blurred/ that its inhabitants are one another." He is flattering them in order to sell more wheelmine stock, and he is quite successful.

Scene Three. Something, however, has happened at the wheelmine in the interim, for some miners have been killed or injured in an accident there. Death, as in the first scene, is strolling, only this time he is masked as Santa. He hears angry voices, and he says in self-satisfaction: "I've got him now!" Santa enters, masked as Death, running from the Mob, and again asks for help. Death assures him that wheelmines don't exist. Then how, asks Santa, can a wheelmine hurt people, turn them into monsters. Because, answers Death, people don't exist either. At this point, Santa suddenly sees who Death is:

D. . . . Now if I may be allowed to analyze—
S.   Do you want to die?
D. I die? Ha-ha-ha-ha! How could Death die?
S. —Death?
D.   Didn't you know?

But Santa is desperate and still needs advice; so Death tells him that what he obviously must do is prove that he (Santa) doesn't exist either. I infer that Death, knowing the Mob will finally take Santa-Scientist to be Death, expects his advice to complete Santa's downfall. For the Mob fears Death and will never believe he doesn't exist.

Death exits, but as it turns out, he hasn't reckoned on the power of the little girl who follows the Mob which has just entered. Santa, who has now seen that he was tricked by Death, tries to explain to the Mob what's wrong:

Ladies and gentlemen: if you all have been
deceived by some impostor—so have I.
If you all have been tricked and ruined—so have I.
And so has every man and woman, I say.
I say it, and you feel it in your hearts:
we are all of us no longer glad and whole,
we have all of us sold our spirits into death,
we are all of us the sick parts of a sick thing,
we have all of us lost our living honesty,
and so we are all of us not any more ourselves.
—who can tell truth from falsehood any more?
I say it, and you feel it in your hearts:
no man or woman on this big small earth.
How should our sages miss the mark of life,
and our most skilful players lose the game?
Your hearts will tell you, as my heart has told me:
because all know, and no one understands.
—O, we are all so very full of knowing
that we are empty: empty of understanding.

Now this is a very direct utterance of what we know Cummings himself believes, and I find it very moving. But it is surrounded by ironies and ends, as we shall see, in a crude joke. In the first place, Santa is telling them just what Death told him in the first scene, only here Santa is lamenting the deadness of mostpeople rather than lampooning it. Notice, secondly, that they have been tricked by Death, however, into giving up their living spirits. If this is so, then we can re-read Death's description of the unworld in the first scene in a new light, a world "so timid, it would rather starve itself/ eternally than run the risk of choking." For here, Death is describing satirically the results of his own handiwork, the same kind of handiwork he tried to exercise in giving Santa false counsel two times over. This sort of allegorical externalization of the fearful and sterile impulses in man which cause him to turn into an idiotic monster of negation is, I think, a new note in Cummings, for he customarily locates those causes within man himself. Now, however, it seems that even Santa Claus can be duped—or has he duped himself? When he learns who Death is, he says:

> I'm going mad. You: tell me,
> whatever you are, Death or the Devil, tell me:
> how can I prove I'm not to blame for the damage
> caused by an accident which never happened
> to people who are nonexistent?

This is the first mention I am aware of in Cummings of the Devil in such a context, and I am not sure whether the necessities of the allegorical form are responsible for this otherwise intelligible externalization, or whether the necessities of a new concept are responsible for the shape of the allegory. I would guess that Cummings does not postulate a power of evil in the universe which lies in wait to trick us, for such a concept would not harmonize with what we know of the rest of his work, and I would tentatively conclude that when Death tricks us it is because we have *allowed* ourselves to be tricked, because like Santa Claus we are not careful of the means we use to attain our desired ends. Death, in this view, embodies not the principle of Evil in the universe, but rather our own sterility. It may be, then, that this beautiful speech of Santa's is further undercut by two more ironies: first, that he is still being deluded when he says we have all been tricked and ruined by Death; and second, that when he tries to give the Mob his understanding, although what he says is true, he is nevertheless wasting his breath. What Death told him in the first scene still applies:

> We are not living in an age of gifts:
> this is an age of salesmanship, my friend;
> and you are heavy with the only thing
> which simply can't be sold.

Santa is still the Reformer, but the Mob will not be reformed, as the outcome demonstrates. But wait—what if this heartfelt speech of Santa's, which sounds like the poet's most impassioned lament over the world, is in reality only one more ruse, this time to fool Death and the Mob at one fell swoop?

At any rate, this is the way the scene ends:

> . . . we are empty: empty of understanding;
> but, by that emptiness, I swear to you . . .
> all men and every woman may be wrong;
> but nobody who lives can fool a child.
> —Now I'll abide by the verdict of that little girl
> over there, with the yellow hair and the blue eyes.
> I'll simply ask her who I am; and whoever
> she says I am, I am: is that fair enough?

The Mob agrees, and the child says, "You are Santa Claus." The Mob laughs, "there ain't no Santa Claus!" Santa is exonerated:

> Then, ladies and gentlemen, I don't exist.
> And since I don't exist, I am not guilty.
> And since I am not guilty, I am innocent.
> —Goodbye! And, next time, look before you leap.

As it turns out, then, Death's advice inadvertently proved, as he says in the next scene, "efficacious."

Scene Four. Santa, still masked as Death, is the one who

is strolling this time, and he is wondering who that child was. Death, still masked as Santa Claus, enters and Santa thanks him for his good advice. But it is Death who asks for a favor now: he has a date with a woman who prefers plump fellows, and asks Santa to give him his fat and take his skeleton in return. Santa agrees, and they exchange costumes. Santa asks him if he has ever loved a woman. "No," says Death. "Have you?" Santa: "Once." Death: "Well, everybody makes mistakes . . . I'll see you later. So long, Mister Death!" Is this why Death's clear insight is diabolic, that he cannot love?

At this point, the child enters and immediately recognizes Santa, in spite of his additional disguise. She says they are both looking for somebody very beautiful and sad; that somebody is sad because she has lost them both. At this point Santa realizes that the child is his and the woman his beloved.

Scene Five. The Woman enters, weeping:

> *Knowledge has taken love out of the world*
> *and all the world is empty empty empty:*
> *men are not men anymore in all the world*
> *for a man who cannot love is not a man,*
> *and only a woman in love can be a woman;*
> *and, from their love alone, joy is born—joy!*
> *Knowledge has taken love out of the world*
> *and all the world is joyless joyless joyless.*

She calls for death, for she has lost her joy and her love and herself. Santa, dressed as Death, enters and speaks; she becomes strangely happy, seeming to hear the voice of her love again. The Mob enters, reeling and capering, carrying on a pole the corpse of Death disguised as Santa Claus. They are exulting over having revenged themselves at last over Science, whom they identify with Santa Claus. Santa disguised as Death fooled them, but Death disguised as Santa didn't, and each time it was the child who was instrumental:

A Voice. He fooled us once, and once was once too much!
Another. He never fooled us, pal: it was the kid.

Another. *Yeah, but the second time—boy, was that good!*
Another. *I'll say it was!*
Another. *Did you see the look she gave him!*
Another. *Did you hear her say "that isn't Santa Claus"?*
Chorus. *Ha-ha-ha-ha—there ain't no Santa Claus!*

What has happened, apparently, is that, while thinking she fooled them the first time, they think that they fooled *her* the second time. She had said that Santa disguised as Death was Santa Claus, and they had let him go. But when she said that Death disguised as Santa *wasn't* Santa Claus, they refused to believe her and killed Death by mistake. And again several ironies confront us: first, that their second disbelief depends upon their first belief, for they wouldn't have assumed their enemy was Santa unless she had identified him for them to begin with; and second, that their real enemy is Death after all.

The play concludes with Santa unmasking and being reunited with the Woman and Child at last.

ii

What does it all add up to? I think the story as a whole can best be understood in the light of the following interpretation: What we see of the action as it is shown in the play itself represents the culmination and failure of a plan on Death's part. He has taken over the world, and only three people remain alive, but they have lost one another. Death tries to ensnare Santa, but is foiled by the child. He then heads for the Woman, for she is the one he has a date with, but is accidentally intercepted by the Mob, and the child is thereupon ironically responsible for his death. The plot, then, of this play is that of the biter bit, or the tables turned, for Death is caught in his own trap. The three are reunited, and the Mob remains the Mob.

It is called a Morality because it deals with representative types and allegorical characters, and because it therefore points a moral. And what is the moral? I suppose in its simplest terms the play says, as Cummings says of Krazy Kat, that the world of *love conquers all* triumphs over the world of *might makes right*. But, as was also the case with Krazy, there's more to it than that. There, we recall, a certain complexity was introduced when Cummings explained the necessity of the brick. Here too, it seems to me, a certain complexity has not yet been accounted for, a complexity deriving from the interchanges of costumes. And this complexity is based, as it was before, upon a central paradox. Cummings' world and Cummings' work are rarely as simple as is sometimes assumed.

We noticed, for example, that when Santa puts on Death's mask, it's himself he fools as well as the Mob, and he's nearly destroyed by the illusion he himself has created. Correspondingly, when Death disguises himself as Santa, it's the Woman he wants to fool, and he *is* destroyed by the illusion he himself has created. But neither Death nor the Mob ever learn anything; it's rather Santa who learns. And what he learns may help us grasp more firmly the play's moral.

It is Death who tells Santa that what he (Santa) has to give is understanding. But what kind of understanding can Santa have if he's deluded by Death into trying to become a knowledge-salesman? On the other hand, Death has a clear insight into the real nature of the unworld as an idiotic monster of negation. But what kind of insight is it if he's the one who, as Santa later tells the Mob, is responsible for the world being that way in the first place? Thus, while the giving-taking, understanding-knowledge, and Santa-Death dichotomies are valid Cummingsesque dichotomies, the play cannot be read simply in these terms.

For there is a third term which is introduced only at the end by the Woman. Compare and contrast Santa's lament with hers:

> S.—O, *we are all so very full of knowing*
> *that we are empty: empty of understanding.*

> W. *Knowledge has taken love out of the world*
> *and all the world is empty empty empty.*

This is the second mention of love in the play, and the difference between these two passages is due to the fact, I think, that until the last scene Santa is alone and has lost his love. That is why he is so easily duped by Death and why his lament to the Mob is so ineffective. He cannot save himself, only the child saves him; he cannot conquer Death, only the child can do that. Thus, although understanding is the proper transcendental alternative to knowledge, it is powerless by itself: it cannot recognize death when it sees it, it does not really understand the world, and it cannot distinguish lies from truth. On the other hand, even though Death can do these things, he too is incomplete. The insight of both, in other words, is only partly true (in opposite ways) because each is without love: Death's is accurate but demonic, while Santa's is well-intentioned but naive.

We might say, in sum, that Santa must become a whole and entire human being through love before his understanding can become effective. That is the meaning of his removal of the deathmask, the moment which Cummings chose to represent in a line drawing intended as the frontispiece of the book. This is his explanation of the drawing in a letter to Allen Tate (June 6, 1946), who apparently was serving as an editor for Holt:

Dear Allen—

here's your (7x9¾) frontispiece

it's a simple linedrawing in leadpencil—
nothing complicated & gaudy—because "Santa
Claus" is neither gaudy nor complicated.
It illustrates the play's almost final
moment—Santa revealing himself to
Woman—because that's the play's climax.
And it symbolizes the whole aim of "Santa
Claus"—which is to make man remove his
deathmask, thereby becoming what he truly
is:a human being
                        . . . If
anyone should ask why only half the face
appears,tell it him or her that the face's

other half is still in the shadow of the
mask(death)

The picture, however, was never used, and Mr. Tate tells
me he cannot remember why.

The moral, then, is not so much that love conquers all
as that the Good as well as the Evil is self-destructive without it.

iii

We have come a long way, via *Tom*, from *Him*.
There were allegorical elements in *Tom*, we noticed, and
the ballet was conceived in obviously spiritual terms. Yet
it did deal primarily with a literal action involving human
beings in trouble. Not so literal as the main action in *Him*,
however, in spite of all its surrealistic interludes, nor so allegorical as *Santa Claus*. Similarly, although each work involves the problem of the human trinity—father, mother,
child—*Santa Claus* is quite different from *Him*, with *Tom*
coming somewhere in between. The unborn baby, we recall, was the main source of strife between the poet-lover
and his lady, in *Him*, whereas here the child is the chief
agent of salvation and reconciliation. There is a similar
reconciliation scene at the end of *Tom*, but the child there
was not the redeemer. There is finally the shift in style
from the sinewy and lyric prose of *Him*, to the nervous
acrobatic notations of *Tom*, to the ceremonial-colloquial
blank verse of *Santa Claus*.

But basically what has happened from 1927 to 1935 to
1946 is that Cummings' moral values and artistic skills
have crystallized and become disciplined. If *Him* has the
organicity of life itself, it is nevertheless persistently ambiguous at its core and its organization does not at every
point seem entirely apt. *Santa Claus* is a beautifully balanced and controlled piece of work, and even though its
moral is paradoxical at the core, it is not ambiguous. It has
almost twenty years of Cummings' growth as a poet behind it. Yet, in order to achieve this artful effect, Cummings had to leave his troubled artist behind and portray

instead a faceless young man wearing masks. If he had ever written another play, and I wish he had, I would have hoped that he could combine the virtues of both these works into one consummate drama.

WHEN CUMMINGS PUBLISHED his first book of poems in the fifties he was fifty-six years old, and when he published his second he was sixty-four. We have therefore reached the full flowering of his development, and these two volumes bear sufficient witness to that fact. Critics who lament Cummings' persistent lack of maturity are simply not reading the words on the page.

Xaipe (pronounced "Khi-ra"), Cummings' third Greek title, means "greetings" or "rejoice!"—or, following a cue from no. 53 which I take to be the title poem, "be thou gay." This volume contains seventy-one poems which are numbered consecutively without being further subdivided. They may, however, be grouped as follows:

1] Satires—contains twelve poems, which represents something of a falling off in relation to the preceding volumes. Indeed, as we shall see when discussing the next book of poems, this trend continues as the poet gets older. This certainly does not mean that there is less folly and error in the world, but perhaps it does mean that Cummings is—not becoming mellower, exactly—becoming rather more absorbed in visionary things. For there is what appears to be a correspondingly greater number of poems embodying transcendental impressions of scenes, people, things, and animals. It is as if he were turning away at last from the dissonances of the so-called real world and concentrating his attention on the harmonies of the natural or actual world.

But not entirely, for there is still plenty of mischief here. Two pieces in particular—no. 24 and no. 46—are bound to kick up a fuss, for one uses the word "nigger" and the other the word "kike." Here is the first (a442 *):

> one day a nigger
> caught in his hand
> a little star no bigger
> than not to understand
>
> "i'll never let you go
> until you've made me white"
> so she did and now
> stars shine at night

This is a condensed and cryptic tale, and it is likely that Cummings counted too heavily on the reader's ability (1) to think clearly about racial issues and their accompanying languages, and (2) to make inferences about what the poem says on the basis of a sparsely told parable. When I wrote and asked him to comment on this poem, this is what he replied (June 25, 1955):

> an 8line expose of all dogoodery. The poem says: once upon a time, when stars shone by day, a blackman—who (being incapable of self-understanding) could only see-&-resent his own blackness in terms of the non-black ("white") ness of what EMForster (in A Passage To India) aptly calls the pinko-grey race—caught a star in his hand & told her "i'll never let you go until you make me white": "So she did" make him "white"; & "now stars shine at night"
>
> when the skies fall, we'll all catch larks (old saw)

It would seem, then, that the stars shining at night represent a diminishment as a result of the blackman's mistaken choice, for they were once bright enough to shine by day. The point is, obviously, that Cummings wants the Negro to be himself, that for the Negro to want to become white is a loss rather than an improvement. And for dogooders to want to rescue the Negro from his blackness by making him white like themselves—that is, respectable and middle-class—is the ultimate in condescension. For if equality is an ideal, shouldn't it work both ways?

The use of the word "nigger" is clearly a risky thing, for even *Huckleberry Finn* has been banned from library shelves by dogooders who object to the term. But what they fail to face is the fact that it is a real word and so is fair game for a writer. Like many such terms, "nigger" can be used in at least three different ways: (1) as a term of contempt, used by one who considers himself superior, whether black or white; (2) as a term of endearment, used by one who is on affectionate and intimate terms, whether black or white; and (3) as a neutral and descriptive term. Certainly it is hard, and hardly desirable, to keep these uses distinct, nor does Cummings—much less Twain—attempt to do so. If we are not overly self-conscious, we can accept the word in this poem in its neutral sense, but we can also accept it in its other senses as well: Cummings disparages the black man who wants to be white, and yet he obviously feels affection for him too, for in wanting him to be himself, Cummings implies that he has a self worth being (compare his ballet, *Tom*). He also implies, by the same token, that being white is not necessarily the epitome of human nobility.

Here is the second poem (a454 *):

> *a kike is the most dangerous*
> *machine as yet invented*
> *by even yankee ingenu*
> *ity(out of a jew a few*
> *dead dollars and some twisted laws)*
> *it comes both prigged and canted*

And here are two comments on it by Cummings. The first is from a letter to Allen Tate (July 20, 1945), to whom he had sent this poem along with six others for Tate's editorial consideration:

> quite incidentally:anyone who resents 3 on the unground that it's "antiJewish" must either be méchant or eed-yoh —since my Good American point = that the kike isn't

> (hélas) a Jew—so heraus mit said objector. But if
> someone won't print "pricked and cunted" which is sexual,
> and will print "pr-cked and c-nted" which is obscene,
> ça m'est égal

This last sentence told me something I never suspected before, although I'm sure the sexual punning of the final version has always been recognized by careful readers. It seems to me that the earlier version, as suggested by this letter, is much inferior, and that the published poem, in being richer and less explicit, represents a happy improvement.

The second comment is quoted by Charles Norman (p. 344):

> Whereas in unpopular parlance 'a kike' equals a jew, for me 'a kike' equals an UNjew. Why? Because for me a jew is a human being; whereas 'a kike' is a machine—the product of that miscalled Americanization, alias standardization (id est dehumanization) which, from my viewpoint,- makes out&out murder a relatively respectable undertaking.

I think the trouble is the same here, that the poem uses inflammatory material in too condensed and cryptic a fashion. Cummings is trying to break through the stereotypes—both liberal and nonliberal—embodied in these terms, and yet the effect on many readers is just the reverse of that intended. But the blame must be shared by these readers as well, for the poem's meaning *is* clear when read attentively: a kike is what Americanization makes out of a Jew, just as a nigger is what wanting to become white makes out of a Negro. It's a reduction from individualism to mass society, a loss all around. Once such a stereotype has been made—in this case, out of a Jew, his not entirely justified reputation as a rich banker, and the misrepresentation of some of his laws—it no longer has any human content and can easily be led to the gas ovens. Of course, things never came to this pass in America, but the cant of U. S. prigs has the same roots as the genocide of otherwise respectable Germans.

The remaining satires include an obscene invective against Franklin Delano Roosevelt, a bitter reaction to American militarism, a puzzling description of what I take to be a Babbitt, a war satire, a portrait of a diminutive general, a protest against America's silence at the Russian invasion of Finland, a blast at generals and admirals, a wry comment on our wartime alliance with Stalin, an epigram on Mr. Universe, and a protest against the destructiveness of modern warfare (37, 38, 39, 40, 42, 43, 44, 45, 47, 49). Most of these satires, then, appear to have grown out of the wreck of the forties.

2] Impressions—contains twenty-nine poems, or almost half of the book. These fall into four groups: visionary scenes, people, things, and animals. The first group contains several of Cummings' many transcendental descriptions of the transition from sunset to evening and of the emergence of the moon and the stars, a picture of a discovered rose, of lovers by the seashore, and of the awakening of spring (1, 3, 5, 10, 35, 41, 65, 71).

The second group describes people in twilight, two old men dreaming on a park bench, a child, an oriental dancer, a tramp wandering down Conway Street, people emerging drunkenly from a bar into the snow, a mysterious encounter with a Christ-like Joe Gould, a country woman in a pasture, a man sharpening a scytheblade, and a bum going through a park (2, 12, 14, 17, 18, 31, 50, 56, 58, 64).

The third presents the city seen in a broken mirror lying in the street, nine birds rising in the wintry twilight, the arrival of snow, a cast-off Christmas tree, the opening of a rose, and the falling of a soft country rain (25, 29, 30, 32, 34, 48, 55).

The fourth describes a young elephant, a cat jumping, and a newly-born horse. (33, 57, 59).

By and large, these poems embody a world which is the antithesis of that of the satires, and the gradual increase of rural scenes is a significant trend whose development we will trace in the next book. Furthermore, there is in these two books a resurgence of interest in typographical experimentation, which appears to be directly related to the increased emphasis upon description (a458, no. 55 *):

* Copyright, 1950, by E. E. Cummings and reprinted by permission of Harcourt, Brace & World, Inc.

```
(fea
therr
ain

:dreamin
g field o
ver forest &;

wh
o could
be

so
!f!
te

r?n
oo
ne)
```

3] Transcendentalism—contains eleven poems, which brings us back to the sort of poem whose emergence we discussed in connection with *No Thanks*, the poem devoted to transcendental statement. It is here, of course, that Cummings' development appears most explicitly, for a poet who explores continuously the meaning of timelessness cannot be viewed as a perennial adolescent, particularly one for whom death becomes an increasingly interesting subject as he grows older (a431–32, no. 6 *):

```
dying is fine)but death

?o
baby
i

wouldn't like

Death if Death
were
good:for
```

when(instead of stopping to think)you

begin to feel of it,dying
's miraculous
why?be

cause dying is

perfectly natural;perfectly
putting
it mildly lively(but

Death

is strictly
scientific
& artificial &

evil & legal)

we thank thee
god
almighty for dying

(forgive us,o life!the sin of Death

Also found in this group is an appreciation of the multi-plicity of a self, a contrast between nature and society, an allegory about the relation between heart and mind and soul, some observations about time and the seasons, the experience of a transcendental moment, a praise of in-nocence, another poem about death, the title poem al-ready mentioned, a poem about the visionary world itself, and another contrast between nature and civilization (11, 22, 23, 27, 36, 51, 52, 53, 54, 60).

4] Love—contains seven poems. There are again fewer love poems in the fifties, as there were in the thirties, but it's hard to cut a clean line between love poems and tran-scendental poems. If they were classified together, they would form a full and constant trend from the mid-thirties on, and perhaps that's the best way of viewing them. Where, however, it seems possible to make the division, I

have made it for the sake of whatever additional light may
be thrown thereby on Cummings' development. Praise of
the lady's hair, for example, seems to call for special comment, as does the comic poem about boys and the girls
they prefer, and the serious and transcendental love sonnets and songs which are one of the main features of this
book (15, 21, 61, 66, 67, 68, 69). The last three but one
make remarkable use of syntactical dislocation and phrasal
balance to create musical effects. Number 66, for instance,
has four six-line stanzas, and each contains a lovely variation on the same refrain (a464–65)

> *that love are in we,that love are in we*
>
> . . . .
> *(for love are in we am in i are in you)*
>
> . . . .
> *for love are in we are in love are in we*
>
> . . . .
> *for love are in you am in i are in we*

Number 67 has three seven-line stanzas with the following
three variations on a refrain (a465):

> *and breathing is wishing and wishing is having—*
>
> . . . .
> *and wishing is having and having is giving—*
>
> . . . .
> *and having is giving and giving is living—*

Number 68 may be quoted in full (a465–66 *):

> *love our so right*
> *is,all(each thing*
> *most lovely)sweet*
> *things cannot spring*
> *but we be they'll*
>
> *some or if where*
> *shall breathe a new*
> *(silverly rare*
> *goldenly so)*
> *moon,she is you*

> *nothing may,quite*
> *your my(my your*
> *and)self without,*
> *completely dare*
> *be beautiful*
>
> *one if should sing*
> *(at yes of day)*
> *younger than young*
> *bird first for joy,*
> *he's i he's i*

The lover is telling his lady that the perfection of nature requires the presence of their love, so right is that love. Thus the spring becomes them, the moon becomes her, and the bird becomes him. But the flatness of my prose should serve to heighten the contrast between the ordinary way of saying these things and Cummings' way. Part of the difference, of course, is created by the rhyming syllabics out of which he builds his stanzas. But more than this, the disarrangement of syntax and the balancing of phrases are responsible for the special singing effect here. All defies analysis, so inevitable does the whole seem. Except for the third stanza, which doesn't seem to fit the pattern and which has a graceless explanatory function; its first three lines seem to me to be especially clumsy and do not sing at all. Indeed, this is one of the besetting sins of Cummings' mature style: where in his youth he had verbal flamboyance, the danger was his habit of clotting and packing his lines with pyrotechnics; where in his maturity he has clarity and luminous balance, the danger is his occasional lapse into a mechanical line or two made up out of his code words, or simply into prosaic flatness.

5] Portraits, Elegies, and Praise—contains eleven poems, which brings us back to an interest in people which began in *No Thanks*, rose to a high in *50 Poems*, and subsided a while in *1 x 1*. This interest, implying as it does a man who is aware of others, with admired friends and with friends who die, is another sign of maturity which many critics have chosen to ignore. The subjects are an organ grinder, Peter Munro Jack, Paul Rosenfeld, Ford Madox Ford, a Chinese laundryman, Aristide Maillol, an ice-coal-wood man, a knife sharpener, an admired autumnal lady, a mender of things, and Chaucer (4, 7, 8, 9, 13, 19, 20, 26, 28, 62, 63). My favorite is no. 26, the one about the knife sharpener (a443 *):

> *who sharpens every dull*
> *here comes the only man*
> *reminding with his bell*
> *to disappear a sun*
>
> *and out of houses pour*
> *maids mothers widows wives*
> *bringing this visitor*
> *their very oldest lives*
>
> *one pays him with a smile*
> *another with a tear*
> *some cannot pay at all*
> *he never seems to care*
>
> *he sharpens is to am*
> *he sharpens say to sing*
> *you'd almost cut your thumb*
> *so right he sharpens wrong*
>
> *and when their lives are keen*
> *he throws the world a kiss*
> *and slings his wheel upon*
> *his back and off he goes*
>
> *but we can hear him still*
> *if now our sun is gone*
> *reminding with his bell*
> *to reappear a moon*

Almost everything seems to work and sing just right in this poem, one line calling for and being answered by the next, the delicate half-rhymes falling perfectly into place, the code words and metaphors coming out in good order, and the structure of the whole forming a concise and rounded little narrative. But there is one, perhaps two weak spots: the last two lines of the third stanza and the last two of the fifth seem flatter than the high standard set by the rest of the poem:

> . . . *some cannot pay at all*
> *he never seems to care*

> . . . *and slings his wheel upon*
> *his back and off he goes*

The rest, however, is faultless, especially the way in which the last stanza echoes and varies the first with an inevitable rightness of image and rhythm.

ii

Eight years later Cummings published *95 Poems,* the second book whose title refers simply to the number of poems within. And a remarkable book it is for a poet to have brought out in his sixty-fourth year, for the windows of perception have been cleansed, and the satirical vision has been practically replaced by crystal-clear impressions of nature and a consistently maturing transcendentalism. If it is true that Cummings is a poet of nature and of love, it is only partly true: the real fact of the matter is that he is these things only in the sense that they are parts of that basic mystical insight which is the real foundation of his work. And this insight is no longer simply a question of the false routine world in opposition to the true or actual world; the true or actual world is now being seen by a poet who feels the weight of mortality and the nearness of death, and there is in this book, therefore, a new complexity of vision, a new sense of the cost of transcendence. And yet, perhaps because of this, of the felt sense of the heavy obstacles overcome, Cummings' affirmations were never more strong. Surely, there is an *artistic* gain here as well, for this kind of contrast serves to maximize the impact of affirmation, and paradox becomes at last a fully mastered device.

The poems in this book are numbered consecutively and

are not grouped in any way. But we may follow our customary scheme for the sake of discussion and analysis:

1] Satire, Comedy, and Comment—contains nine poems, which really represents a low point. From *is 5* until *1 x 1* satires had formed from a quarter to a third of each book of poems, but now they form barely a tenth. And even this tenth is not in the old manner—except for no. 39, the "THANKSGIVING (1956)" attack on America's official indifference to the Soviet suppression of the Hungarian revolution. This is one of the two disappointments for me in *95 Poems*, and they are both strangely connected with the problems Cummings had over the Boston Fine Arts Festival in June of 1957 (see Norman, pp. 358–68). He was asked to read at this Festival, and he chose "THANKSGIVING" as the featured work. The committee in charge balked, and Cummings finally agreed to replace it by "i am a little church" (which we shall examine shortly), provided that he could read the first poem during the remainder of the reading. Now there is plenty of obscenity in Cummings' satires, and rightly so, but when it becomes merely disagreeable, a question might be raised as to its appropriateness. Here is the penultimate stanza (b, no. 39):

> *uncle sam shrugs his pretty*
> *pink shoulders you know how*
> *and he twitches a liberal titty*
> *and lisps "i'm busy right now"*

The closest thing to this is that other disagreeable poem, the one on FDR in *Xaipe* (a449–50, no. 37):

> *F is for foetus(a*
>
> *punkslapping*
> *mobsucking*
> *gravypissing poppa*

These passages seem to me to be angry without wit. Two similarly obscene passages from *50 Poems* I think are more successful (a357–58, no. 11, and a359–60, no. 14):

> some like it shot
> and some like it hung
> and some like it in the twot
> nine months young

> the way to hump a cow is not
> to get yourself a stool
> but draw a line around the spot
> and call it beautifool

In the first, the indignation is controlled by the parody ("pease porridge hot"), and in the second, it is modified by the humor of the metaphor and the fun of the exaggerated rhyme. But in the Hungary and FDR poems there is nothing but obscene outrage, and this is not art.

As for the rest, they are a mild lot. Some are simply commentaries, and I have placed them here for lack of a better category. Number 10 is a very good poem about "maggie and milly and molly and may" who "went down to the beach(to play one day)," and which concludes:

> For whatever we lose(like a you or a me)
> it's always ourselves we find in the sea

These lines illustrate the new kind of thing Cummings is doing in this book, the switch in meaning created by using the same or similar words in different ways, a switch which reveals a developed sense of how the transcendental world is involved in the ordinary world as well as a maturing grasp of poetic style and technique. A dozen years before this, in writing about Krazy Kat, Cummings concluded that the triumph of spirit was intimately connected with the impact of the brick of reality on the head. And now it is as if that brick had finally entered the world of the poems (b, no. 58 *):

> a total stranger one black day
> knocked living the hell out of me—

> who found forgiveness hard because
> my(as it happened)self he was

* © 1958 by E. E. Cummings and reprinted by permission of Harcourt, Brace & World, Inc.

—but now that fiend and i are such
immortal friends the other's each

Number 17 laments the diminishments people are content to live by, 18 speaks of death, 57 comments wryly on the opposition and ultimate reconciliation of youth and age, and 59 does an epigrammatic switch on the opening lines of *Paradise Lost.*

There are, finally, a few comedies. Number 28 does a take-off on Joe Gould's explanation of why women go to college, 29 tells of a woman who doesn't have what it takes, and 35 perpetrates an outrageous pun on "morticians."

2] Impressions—contains forty-eight poems, just over one-half of the entire volume. These may be subdivided into five groups: times, weathers, seasons; city scenes; country scenes; birds; and flowers. If Cummings is a poet of spring, he is also a poet of autumn and winter. The first three poems of the book deal with autumn: no. 1 is one of those opening vertical poems which read like the inscriptions on some Japanese paintings, and describes simply and accurately the loneliness of a leaf falling; no. 2 embodies a moment of transcendence experienced during a fall twilight; and no. 3 represents the breath-taking clarity and freshness of the time between summer and winter, life and death. Many poems involve snow and winter, but three deal with them directly: no. 41 is an appreciation of the snow falling, and the typography helps suggest the timelessness of the experience by printing the word "s/ Now"; no. 43 shows a father and his child looking out of a window at a snowfall; and no. 44 celebrates a snowman. Naturally, spring is not far behind, and there are four poems dealing explicitly with the new season: no. 16 speaks of spring and transcendence, finding the season analogous to that "mystery to be/ (when time from time shall set us free)"; no. 66 celebrates April and her flowers; and nos. 93 and 95 are joyous spring songs. And night, the arrival of the first star, the transcendent heavens, the moon, twilight, and the sun account for eight more poems (47, 48, 49, 50, 51, 61, 78, 84).

There are five city scenes, and these describe a small

empty park in the autumn rain, an encounter with an organ-grinder and his fortune-telling cockatoo, lovers in a park, what appears to be one more barroom brawl, and some American businessmen in a French hotel (24, 25, 26, 34, 36). This group is a far cry from Cummings' early days of street-prowling and night-clubbing. During the first decade of his publishing career he wrote well over fifty poems dealing with gangsters, whores, and the demi-monde in New York, Boston, and Paris. But after 1935 these subjects almost disappeared; in place of crowds and hullabaloo, we now have (except for no. 34) a relatively gentle and lonely city.

What appears to be a strongly developing rural interest, on the other hand, is represented by eight poems: a deserted cellar hole, country tombstones, that country church, an old blue wheel in a pasture, summer rain, lovers in a pasture, and a dark forest pool (21, 23, 77, 81, 82, 83, 85, 86). Cummings had always looked forward to going to his summer home in Silver Lake, New Hampshire, but it was not until recently that the Silver Lake country began making its explicit presence felt in his poetry (he has done many paintings, however, of these environs). But no. 77, the country church poem which finally was featured at the Fine Arts Festival, is my other disappointment. This poem, it seems to me, demonstrates by contrast what Cummings has achieved in coining a language of his own, for it contains his own characteristic diction side by side with some of the most mawkish and sentimental lines and phrases to be found anywhere this side of Mr. Vinal. Compare, for example, "children/ whose any sadness or joy is my grief or my gladness," or "merciful Him Whose only now is forever," with:

around me surges a miracle of unceasing
birth and glory and death and resurrection:
over my sleeping self float flaming symbols
of hope . . .

i am a little church(far from the frantic
world with its rapture and anguish)at peace with nature . . .

Never has Cummings called the stars anything like "flaming symbols/ of hope," or referred to the world as "frantic," or used such a perfectly banal phrase as "at peace with nature." I see now how really wrong critics are who have called Cummings sentimental, for this poem is indeed the exception that proves the rule. If he has not always followed his own advice (a167–68, no. II) that

> certain ideas gestures
> rhymes, like Gillette Razor Blades
> having been used and reused
> to the mystical moment of dullness emphatically are
> Not To Be Resharpened.

—he has *almost* always followed it. Here, however, something went wrong.

Birds and flowers seem somehow to have gained in interest for the maturing poet, and these are clearly related to his fresh and awakening view of the countryside, all of which constitutes a distinctive feature of this volume. I can't recall so many bird poems in any previous book: there are ten of them here. In one, a blue jay is saluted as a "beautiful anarchist"; in another, a phoebe's winter courage is admired; in a third, a group of huddling birds sitting on a twig is seen against a cold moon; in a fourth, a bird is seen watching the fall turn into winter; in another, a robin greets the spring; in yet another, robins are seen as household guardians against hate and fear; in a seventh, a pair of hummingbirds twitter; in an eighth, a whippoorwill calls over the noonday hills; in another, a bird sings the Lovestar under the earth at night; and in the last, a transcendental birdsong is celebrated (5, 6, 15, 40, 65, 74, 75, 79, 80, 87).

And what shall we say of flowers? There are six poems in this group, and the first (no. 12) is a puzzling allegory embodied largely in a conversation between "lily" and "violet" about a rose that lily's lover gave her. It seems that violet is jealous, and her lament which concludes the poem illustrates the new intensity of paradox which characterizes *95 Poems* throughout:

> *lily has a rose*
> *no rose i've*
> *and losing's less than winning(but*
> *love is more than love)*

The other poems show a bee in a rose, the truth of a violet, the meaning of roses, the heavenly glory of white roses from the poet's mother's greatgrandmother's rosebush, and the transcendental symbolism of a rose tree (64, 72, 76, 90). And finally, somewhere in this group belongs no. 20, a poem describing a fly spinning off a windowpane.

In order to understand and appreciate the significance of these forty-eight "impressions," we have to go back to my introductory explanation of Cummings' mystic vision, and then survey his work from the beginning until now. His transcendentalism is not Platonic but Coleridgian; the eternal forms are embodied in the phenomenal universe, and they are embodied as process rather than result. Nature, then, is the alpha and omega of such a view, and the poet's function — regarding both insight and technique — is to capture the dynamic flux of actuality and to embody it in artistic form. Cummings' first poetic decade, as we have seen, was devoted largely to ingesting large hunks of the world and finding a language to match it. His second decade was mainly a matter of seeing within this world to the visionary core. In the third decade, the image of the actual world faded in favor of the visionary core. And now, in the fourth decade, the world has returned, only now it has been fully transformed, image and idea inextricably fused (b, no. 90):

> *rosetree,rosetree*
> *—you're a song to see:whose*
> *all(you're a sight to sing)*
> *poems are opening,*
> *as if an earth was*
> *playing at birthdays. . . .*

3] Transcendentalism — contains four poems, which seems like a falling off, but the next group of love poems shows a corresponding increase since *Xaipe*. The first is about time and timelessness, the second advises the reader to forsake the routine world for the dream or actual world, the third tells of the speaker's transcendence, and the fourth discusses the relation between death and beauty (11, 60, 63, 70). As he grows older the poet finds that time has "generosities beyond believing" (11), that "more he gives than takes" (78); yet he also finds that "he takes all" (78), and "there is a time for timelessness" (11). One of the most beautiful poems Cummings has ever written, which also happens to be one of his loveliest sonnets, is no. 63: *

> *precisely as unbig a why as i'm*
> *(almost too small for death's because to find)*
> *may,given perfect mercy,live a dream*
> *larger than alive any star goes round*
>
> *—a dream sans meaning (or whatever kills)*
> *a giving who(no taking simply which)*
> *a marvel every breathing creature feels*
> *(but none can think)a learning under teach—*
>
> *precisely as unbig as i'm a why*
> *(almost too small for dying's huge because)*
> *given much mercy more than even the*
> *mercy of perfect sunlight after days*
>
> *of dark,will climb;will blossom:will sing(like*
> *april's own april and awake's awake)*

As we know, Cummings prefers questions to answers because questions are open and answers are closed; thus the speaker is a "why" and death is "because." If he is given perfect mercy, such a small person may live in a transcendental world bigger than any merely physical universe. This is a world without any intellectual meaning, incapable of being killed by abstraction; a world of giving rather than taking; a marvel to be felt but not thought, a lesson which can be learned but not taught. If he is given a mercy beyond that of sun after storm, spring after winter, such a small person will transcend, just as the April of April, the awake of awake, transcends. The diction, the phrasal balance and variation, the rhythm, the structure, and above all, the concluding couplet—all work in perfect harmony together. (I'm not sure, however, whether Cummings' strange use of "sans" as if it were a perfectly normal American-English word serves his poetic purpose here. And he uses it several times elsewhere.)

4] Love—contains fifteen poems. The lover praises his lady for giving him the courage to transcend; he reminds her that their "doom is/ to grow . . . not/ only/ wherever the sun and the stars and/ the/ moon/ are . . . but/ also/ nowhere"; he marvels that time and space bow to the lovers; he tells her he loves her so much that the true time of year is spring even in winter; he sends her a valentine; he wittily ponders the meaning of home; he sends her a birthday card; he tells her of death, "most the amazing miracle of all," as they stand in the dusk and watch the stars come out; he tells her of timelessness as they stand by the sea; he invites her to climb the mountains where thrushes sing and where they'll find the "now and here of freedom" far "from some loud unworld's most rightful wrong"; he tells her that by the miracle of her love she makes the unworld disappear; he tells her to look up, "above/ anybody and fate and even Our/ whisper it Selves"; he praises love for giving eternity to lovers; he tells his lady he carries her heart in his; and he describes love's beginninglessness and endlessness (7, 14, 22, 45, 46, 56, 62, 69, 71, 73, 88, 89, 91, 92, 94).

There are twenty sonnets in 95 Poems, and over half of them are transcendental and love poems. In fact, the love poems are almost all transcendental poems. Let none complain any longer that it's nothing but cloying love-love in Cummings, and a pretty vague romanticism at that. For him, love is a real experience and has a definite meaning; and it has very little to do, here in his maturity, with Elizabethan or Cavalier eroticism, or with Romantic or Victorian cloudiness. The force, the depth, and the intensity of the emotion in these poems are unmatched in all of modern poetry, and no equal can be found for them except perhaps in the love poems of John Donne. This is not the prettiness of Elizabeth Barrett Browning, the fleshly mysticism of Rossetti, or the naughtiness of Edna St. Vincent Millay. This is the full and free expression of the passion of a mature artist (b, no. 94):

> *being to timelessness as it's to time,*
> *love did no more begin than love will end;*
> *where nothing is to breathe to stroll to swim*
> *love is the air the ocean and the land*
>
> *(do lovers suffer?all divinities*
> *proudly descending put on deathful flesh:*
> *are lovers glad?only their smallest joy's*
> *a universe emerging from a wish)*
>
> *love is the voice under all silences,*
> *the hope which has no opposite in fear;*
> *the strength so strong mere force is feebleness:*
> *the truth more first than sun more last than star*
>
> *—do lovers love?why then to heaven with hell.*
> *Whatever sages say and fools,all's well*

5] People—contains fourteen poems, which sustains the high level of interest in others set at the beginning of the decade by *Xaipe*. A man is celebrated whose heart is so true to his earth that he can guess exactly what life will do; an ice-coal-wood man, perhaps the same one who appears in no. 20 of *Xaipe*, is shown with a doll wired to the radiator of his truck; a shy, wrong, gay, young man is praised; a cheerful blindman is wonderingly recalled; a man whose life was a failure is pondered; a drunken pencil-vendor is shown staggering up some streetful of people; a platinum floozey is seen regarding herself in a mirror; another drunk is shown boasting; a third drunk is heard mumbling; a little old lady is seen sewing at an open window; another old lady is shown hurling crumbs at some sparrows; a second floozey is distastefully described; a little girl is shown bursting with the inexpressible numberlessness of her selves; and a child's eyes are described (4, 8, 13, 27, 30, 31, 32, 33, 38, 52, 53, 54, 67, 68).

It occurs to me that many of these cast-offs and transcendent individuals are in effect more Delectable Mountains, gentle and mysterious people of the sort celebrated over thirty-five years earlier in *The Enormous Room*. We recall that the young poet had said, toward the end of that book, that "In the course of the next ten thousand years it may be possible to find Delectable Mountains without going to prison . . . it may be possible, I dare say, to encounter Delectable Mountains who are not in prison" (p. 307). If I am right, it was possible even sooner, for surely Dominic Depaola is worthy of a place beside The Wanderer, Zoo-Loo, Surplice, and Jean Le Nègre (b, no. 8 *):

> dominic has
>
> a doll wired
> to the radiator of his
> ZOOM DOOM
>
> icecoalwood truck a
>
> wistful little
> clown
> whom somebody buried
>
> upsidedown in an ashbarrel so
>
> of course dominic
> took him
> home
>
> & mrs dominic washed his sweet
>
> dirty
> face & mended
> his bright torn trousers (quite
>
> as if he were really her &

she
but) & so
that

's how dominic has a doll

& every now & then my
wonderful
friend dominic depaola

gives me a most tremendous hug

knowing
i feel
that

we & worlds

are
less alive
than dolls &

dream

CUMMINGS DID NOT easily face an audience. He never compromised his writing for the sake of the reader, nor did he compromise when on the platform and actually facing people. When he was scheduled to give a reading, his arrival was preceded by a series of instructions from his agent designed to insure as far as possible the poet's physical and psychological comfort. Because of an arthritic back, for example, he found it hard to stand for any length of time and so a chair and desk had to be provided, and a reading lamp was to accompany the desk. So that people would not confuse him with Elvis Presley, as he said, he refused to give autographs. This was not mere crankiness, however: he gave a reading at the University of Connecticut a few years ago, and when one of my students—a charming young lady—seemed disappointed at being refused an autograph, he gallantly and wittily redeemed the situation by impulsively seizing her hand and kissing it. I am sure this meant more to her than his signature!

It was hard, nevertheless, for a man such as this to face crowds of people. Critics have complained of the way he appears to affirm himself by rejecting mostpeople, and, although I think this can be made too much of, there *is* something to the charge. But I don't think Cummings' attitude was arrogant or snobbish: not only was he devoted to his friends, but also people who had gotten to know him are almost unanimous in their praise of his gentle friendliness and courtesy. When people baited him, however, or asked stupid questions, he was apt to become waspish and rude. It is not simply that he was, as he says of his mother, constitutionally shy and so had built up a set of defenses—as any man must who is much in the public eye. It is more that he was preternaturally sensitive to the ubiquity of mostpeople, and so he tended to become edgy when facing a crowd. And who is to blame him for this? Most of his critics, who are used to lecturing and teaching, in all probability have become inured to the fact that audiences and students are by and large listening, if they listen at all, for entertainment or credits and don't really care about what's being said. It may even be that some of this indifference rubs off on the critics themselves, so that in time, before they realize it, *they* don't really care about what's being said either.

Another very well known poet came recently to the University of Connecticut to give a reading, and I spent part of the afternoon and most of the evening in his company. He chatted with students, gave his reading, answered questions from the audience, had cocktails afterwards with some faculty members and their wives, and all in all appeared alert and agreeable. But I felt, as the time wore on, that we were not touching him at all, that he was somewhere else, and that the man we thought we were dealing with was actually just a machine which had been turned on for the occasion. And then I reflected, not without some sadness, that he—and many other widely-traveled writers like him—must have to do this all the time simply in order to protect himself from the weariness of change and the bewilderment of overmuch human contact.

Cummings was not a teacher, however, and when he was asked to conduct a course at Harvard during his tenure (1952–53) as Charles Eliot Norton Professor—the occasion for his six nonlectures—he refused. But he did, as usual, prepare his readings with great care. When he traveled and gave readings from his own work, he planned his program with a view to balance and variety, he recited slowly and distinctly, he gave his audience an intermission, and he put himself entirely into the performance. When he came to Connecticut, I picked him up at the airport. The flight had been delayed for several hours, and by the time the additional hour's drive to the campus had been accomplished, I was rather tired myself. He stretched himself out on a bed in my apartment for a few minutes, with a heating pad under his back, had dinner, and then gave a splendid reading which lasted for an hour and a half.

My point is that, although Cummings did not act like an ordinary celebrity, he did give his audiences their money's worth. I remember when, in the winter 1951/ spring 1952 season, Professor John Finley (in one of whose Humanities courses I was serving as a Teaching Fellow) told me that he was trying to get Cummings to fill the Norton chair for the following year. The poet in the meantime was searching his soul and canvassing his friends for their opinions. I for one wrote him that I thought the Harvard audience would be most interested in himself and his stance as a writer. He finally agreed to accept the offer, and one of the conditions was that he would be allowed to stay in New Hampshire until after the leaves turned in the fall. The customary desk, chair, and lamp were provided: but he did wear a tuxedo! During the summer, then, he worked painstakingly on the manuscript of his nonlectures (p. 3):

> Let me cordially warn you, at the opening of these socalled lectures, that I haven't the remotest intention of posing as a lecturer. Lecturing is presumably a form of teaching; and presumably a teacher is somebody who knows. I never did, and still don't, know. What has always fascinated me is not teaching, but learning; and I assure you that if the acceptance of a Charles Eliot Norton professorship hadn't rapidly entangled itself with the expectation of learning a very great deal, I should now be somewhere else. Let me also assure you that I feel extremely glad to be here; and that I heartily hope you won't feel extremely sorry.

i

And what of the purpose and plan of these nonlectures? Cummings, under his lamp and in his tuxedo, facing the world from the stage of Sanders Theatre, and reading carefully from his manuscript, first laid down the ground rules (p. 3):

> For while a genuine lecturer must obey the rules of mental decency, and clothe his personal idiosyncrasies in collectively acceptable generalities, an authentic ignoramus remains quite indecently free to speak as he feels. This prospect cheers me, because I value freedom; and have never expected freedom to be anything less than indecent.

True to his title, he will speak personally—and he will speak of himself. He is "attempting an aesthetic strip-tease," "trying to tell you who I am," "the self of the prose and of the poetry" (p. 3). What this means, as it turns out, is that he will tell us about his life and work as they reveal what he believes in. This book is less an autobiography than it is a testament of faith, a witness to a vision of life.

Accordingly, his six nonlectures fall into two equal parts (p. 4):

> Inspecting my autobiographical problem at close range, I see that it comprises two problems; united by a certain wholly mysterious moment which signifies selfdiscovery. Until this mysterious moment, I am only incidentally a writer: primarily I am the son of my parents and whatever is happening to him. After this moment, the question "who am I?" is answered by what I write—in other words, I become my writing; and my autobiography becomes the exploration of my stance as a writer.

The entire set of nonlectures is concerned primarily with Cummings' values, for his self is equated with what he stands for. "As a human being stands, so a human being is" (p. 63). Thus the first three tell how he grew to learn these values, while the last three show how they function in his writings.

The first, which is entitled "i & my parents," deals with the poet's father and mother, and affirms that "personality is a mystery; that mysteries alone are significant; and that love is the mystery-of-mysteries who creates them all" (p. 43). Cummings, who had almost reached his sixtieth year at this time, felt nothing but filial piety for his parents, for they had been real people, heroic in their way and true individuals. Perhaps this fact reverses the classical psychological dictum, for Cummings was a rebel not because he found the world a paradigm of his rejected home but rather because he was astonished to find it so different.

The second nonlecture, entitled "i & their son," contrasts "the collective behaviour of unchildren with the mystery of individuality" and gives "one particular child's earliest glimpse of a mystery called nature" (p. 43). He begins with a definition of the idea of home ("the idea of privacy") as opposed to that of a modern house ("to admit whatever might otherwise remain outside"), and continues with an exhortation to those who would be poets: "you've got to forget all about punishments and all about rewards and all about selfstyled obligations and duties and responsibilities etcetera ad infinitum and remember one thing only: that it's you—nobody else—who determine your destiny and decide your fate. Nobody else can be alive for you; nor can you be alive for anybody else" (p. 24). He then speaks of his professorial neighbors; his maternal uncle George, who gave him a book on verseforms; his three poetic periods; the four Cambridge schools he attended; his explorations in "sinful Somerville"; and his adventures in Norton's Woods.

Speaking of the contrast between "a virtuous Cambridge"—whose social stratifications and whose "soi-disant respectability comprised nearly everything which I couldn't respect," although as a professor's (and later a clergyman's) son he "had every socalled reason to accept these distinctions without cavil"—and rough-and-tumble Somerville, he says (pp. 31–32):

> Little by little and bruise by teacup, my doubly disillusioned spirit made an awe-inspiring discovery; which (on more than several occasions) has prevented me from wholly misunderstanding socalled humanity: the discovery, namely, that all groups, gangs, and collectivities—no matter how apparently disparate—are fundamentally alike; and that

what makes any world go round is not the trivial difference between a Somerville and a Cambridge, but the immeasurable difference between either of them and individuality. . . . Nor will anything ever persuade me that by turning Somerville into Cambridge or Cambridge into Somerville or both into neither, anybody can make an even slightly better world. Better worlds (I suggest) are born, not made; and their birthdays are the birthdays of individuals.

And he quotes Blake to explain why he is not a Reformer or a Utopian (p. 32):

Let us pray always for individuals; never for worlds. "He who would do good to another" cries the poet and painter William Blake "must do it in Minute Particulars"—and probably many of you are familiar with this greatly pitying line. But I'll wager that not three of you could quote me the line which follows it

General Good is the plea of the scoundrel, hypocrite, & flatterer

for that deeply terrible line spells the doom of all unworlds; whatever their slogans and their strategies, whoever their heroes or their villains.

That he is not an Anarchist either, however, is evidenced by his story of his first encounter with "that mystery who is Nature," for between "cerebral Cambridge and orchidaceous Somerville" lay "a mythical domain of semiwilderness" called Norton's woods. Nature is, of course, the literal and symbolic alternative to "turning Somerville into Cambridge or Cambridge into Somerville or both into neither," for she has "an illimitable being" and "mortally immortal complexities of . . . beyond imagining imagination" (p. 32). And Cummings concludes this nonlecture with a eulogy of spring.

The third, which is called "i & selfdiscovery," revolves around the climactic turning point of Cummings' life and of the series, telling of "certain attitudes and reactions surrounding the mystery of transition from which emerged a poet and painter named EECummings" (p. 43). He begins with a diatribe against our modern scramble for security, for he feels the world of his adolescence was so much different, "a rising and striving world; a reckless world, filled with the curiosity of life herself; a vivid and violent world welcoming every challenge; a world worth hating and adoring and fighting and forgiving; in brief, a world which was a world" (p. 43). Then he goes on to tell of his days at Harvard, where he got his first taste of independence, and of his trips into Boston to see the shows at The Old Howard. He celebrates the friends he made at college, and especially Theodore Miller who introduced him to Catullus, Horace, and Sappho, and who gave him a volume of Keats's poems and letters; "Whereupon— deep in those heights of psychic sky which had greeted my boyish escape from moralism—an unknown and unknowable bird began singing" (p. 51).

After Harvard he went to New York, where he breathed "as if for the first time." But the "truly first of first times was . . . still to come. It arrived with a socalled war," when he embarked for France as an ambulance driver and discovered Paris, a discovery which led to his self-discovery (pp. 51–52):

> two realms, elsewhere innately hostile, here cordially co-existed—each (by its very distinctness) intensifying the other—nor could I possibly have imagined either a loveliness so fearlessly of the moment or so nobly beautiful a timelessness. Three thousand oceanic miles away and some terrestrial years before, a son of New England had observed those realms bitterly struggling for dominion: then, as a guest of verticality [in New York], our impuritan had attended the overwhelming triumph of the temporal realm. Now, I participated in an actual marriage of material with immaterial things; I celebrated an immediate reconciling of spirit and flesh, forever and now, heaven and earth. Paris was for me precisely and complexly this homogeneous duality: this accepting transcendence; this living and dying more than death or life.

From this moment on, Cummings became a true Paradoxer, one who perceives the soul only through the body, victory only through defeat, and social order only through individual freedom. For what he found in Paris was simply the presence, the "miraculous presence, not of mere children and women and men, but of living human beings" (pp. 52–53):

> While (at the hating touch of some madness called La Guerre) a once rising and striving world toppled into withering hideously smithereens, love rose in my heart like a sun and beauty blossomed in my life like a star. Now, finally and first, I was myself: a temporal citizen of eternity; one with all human beings born and unborn.

It is curious, however, that he chose not to mention at this point his imprisonment at La Ferté Macé, but I think it's because he wanted to end his nonlecture on an affirmative note.

ii

The fourth, entitled "i & you & is," begins the second half of the series, that dealing with the embodiment of these transcendental values, "mysteries" as he calls them, in his writings. "Now comes," he says, "from my point of view, the excitement. . . . an exploration of [my] stance as a writer. Writing, I feel, is an art; and artists, I feel are human beings. As a human being stands, so a human being is. . . . the present non-poetical period will consist of nothing but sentences, essays, and parts of essays, all of which express a standing human being" (63). These last three nonlectures are related as follows: this one (the fourth) presents "one particular individual's purely personal values" abstractly, by means of explicit statements; the fifth presents them concretely as they function in *Him*; and the sixth tests "those complementary aspects of a soi-disant world known as communism and capitalism" by means of these values (p. 79).

And what are they? They "concern themselves," as Cummings says, "with being and with growing" (p. 79). So he reads a passage from *The Enormous Room*, the Foreword to *is 5*, the Imaginary Dialogue from the bookjacket of *Him*, a passage from *Eimi*, a portion of the Introduction to the Modern Library edition of *The Enormous Room*, some passages from the Introduction to the 1938 *Collected Poems*. And here he interrupts his "egocentric self" to read "a pitying and terrible passage from the New Testament," because his next selection is based on it. The passage consists of the first eleven verses of John, viii, those concerning the reaction of Jesus to the woman taken in adultery. Cummings calls this passage "this more than most famous manifestation of whatever I can only call feeling—as against unfeeling: alias knowing and believing and thinking—this masterpoem of human perception, whose seventh verse alone exterminates all conventional morality." That verse is, of course: "So when they continued asking him, he lifted up himself, and said unto them, He that is without sin among you, let him first cast a stone at her" (pp. 66–67).

His next selection, the one based on this passage, is "one of a pair of essays concerning Ezra Pound," and it was written in 1940 for the Gotham Book Mart catalogue entitled *We Moderns*. I must confess that this short piece is rather orphic, and I will have to return to Pound shortly. I suspect, however, that Cummings is questioning the right of the United States to pass judgment on Pound. There follows an essay prefacing the catalogue of an exhibition of Cummings' paintings at the American British Art Center in New York during 1944, an essay "whose subject isn't the art of painting and is Art Herself." Here he denies the civilized categories derived from knowing and measuring as opposed to feeling, categories such as "good" and "bad," "peace" and "war" (p. 68):

> Art is a mystery.
> A mystery is something immeasurable.
> In so far as every child and woman and man may be immeasurable,art is the mystery of every man and woman and child. In so far as a human being is an artist,skies and mountains and oceans and thunderbolts and butterflies are immeasurable;and art is every mystery of nature. Nothing measurable can be alive;nothing which is not alive can be art;nothing which cannot be art is true:and everything untrue doesn't matter a very good God damn.

This may help explain the next selection: the second essay on Pound, written in 1945 for Charles Norman's symposium in *PM*. Cummings introduces this passage by saying it concerns "this selfstyled world's greatest and most generous literary figure: who had just arrived at our nation's capitol, attired in half a GI uniform and ready to be hanged as a traitor by the only country which ever made even a pretense of fighting for freedom of speech." The point of this brief essay is that the artist is not to be judged by the ordinary categories of civilization, which are "dedicated to the proposition that massacre is a social virtue because murder is an individual vice." He is to be judged rather according to whether or not he is true to himself, for "Every artist's strictly illimitable country is himself" (p. 69). But, it might be asked, doesn't it matter what that self *is* to which the artist must be true? In Cummings' eyes, Pound appears to be some sort of Quaker pacifist or conscientious objector. But is it true that Pound's *Cantos* and his behavior during the War reveal that open and spontaneous responsiveness which Cummings feels is essential to the artist? Isn't it true, rather, that Pound thinks just as much in stereotypes, in terms of "good" and "bad," as does the ordinary person? It is one thing to object to war, but it is surely another to join the enemy while doing so! If society is wrong, that does not mean that Pound is right. I feel that Cummings is simply being overly loyal to a friend at this point, but I do not pretend to know enough about this vexed issue to judge. One thing is clear, even if it only confuses the case further: that Cummings never sympathized with Mussolini or with fascism of any kind.

The next selection is from an essay contributed in the same year to Oscar Williams' anthology called *The War Poets*, and once again Cummings contrasts the lies of civilization—in this case, the propaganda necessary to the war effort—with the truth of art. Then he concludes this nonlecture with a few epigrams from "Jottings," published in *Wake* magazine in 1951, of which my favorite is: "knowledge is a polite word for dead but not buried imagination" (p. 70).

So much for precept; we now turn to the examples. The

fifth nonlecture, called "i & now & him," deals with "three mysteries: love, art, and selftranscendence or growing" (p. 81) as they manifest themselves in *Him*. As he explains, "it would more than delight me if this evening all abstractions which we have so far encountered should take unto themselves life; thus creating those very values. Since the mere abstractions—however various—concern themselves with being and with growing, my hope is that tonight you and I may actually feel what growing and being are" (p. 79). One may talk, in other words, about being and growing, but they will not be tested on the pulses until they are actually demonstrated, and that is the function of art—to exemplify in its very existence these qualities. A work of art, we recall, is not *about* something, it *is* something, a verb rather than a noun. It is, that is to say, moving, organic, and alive, aiming to reproduce in the reader the very feel of the insight or experience being rendered. "Art is every mystery of Nature" because it imitates her. And this is where the poet's vision and his art intersect, because they are both grounded in a transcendental conception of nature; vision and art are, indeed, inseparable, for art is a way of being alive, and being an artist is a way of being human. Since we have already considered *Him* separately and at length, however, as well as Cummings' comments on it here, we may turn now to the sixth and last nonlecture.

This one is entitled "i & am & santa claus," and attempts to test "those complementary aspects of a soi-disant world known as communism and capitalism . . . by one particular individual's purely personal values" (p. 79). As we know, Cummings had already juxtaposed *Eimi* with *The Enormous Room* in his Introduction to the latter book, and here he compares and contrasts *Eimi* in a very interesting way with *Santa Claus*. After reading the Lenin's tomb section of *Eimi*, he says (p. 103):

> So much (or so little) for one major aspect of the inhuman unworld: a fanatical religion of irreligion, conceived by sterile intellect and nurtured by omnipotent nonimagination. From this gruesome apotheosis of mediocrity in the

name of perfectibility, this implacable salvation of all through the assassination of each, this reasoned enormity of spiritual suicide, I turn to a complementary—and if possible even more monstrous—phenomenon. That phenomenon is a spiritually impotent pseudocommunity enslaved by perpetual obscenities of mental concupiscence; and omnivorous social hypocrisy, vomiting vitalities of idealism while grovelling before the materialization of its own deathwish: a soi-disant free society, dedicated to immeasurable generosities of love; but dominated by a mere and colossal lust for knowing, which threatens not simply to erase all past and present and future human existence but to annihilate (in the name of liberty) Life Herself.

What troubles him about the Soviet Union, in other words, is her planned destruction of individuality; but what pains him about the United States, and this is far worse, is its hypocrisy in talking about liberty even while destroying it. The play itself, which, as we have seen, opposes selling knowledge to giving love, shows how paradoxically destructive the unrealities of the knowledgeable power-world and how paradoxically creative the unknowledgeable powerlessness of love can be.

Cummings concludes the entire series by reading Keats's "Ode on a Grecian Urn" and the closing stanzas of Shelley's *Prometheus Unbound*, saying, "Ecstasy and anguish, being and becoming; the immortality of the creative imagination and the indomitability of the human spirit— these are the subjects of my final poetry reading" (pp. 110–11). There can be no doubt, then, that the development of E. E. Cummings as a writer reveals him here, at the apex of his career, as one of our most serious and distinguished representatives of the Romantic tradition, a tradition which, in spite of the death-laments perpetually uttered over its imaginary grave, has more life in it and is responsible for more of the life of twentieth-century literature than many of us have been prepared to recognize. Once we have recognized this, and once we have seen what really lies at the heart's core of Cummings' work, then we will be able to accord him his true place in our literary heritage.

And I can find no more appropriate way of concluding this book than by quoting the final portion of the final nonlecture (pp. 110–11), where Cummings returns at last to the "nonanswerable question" with which he began: "who, as a writer, am I?"

> I am someone who proudly and humbly affirms that love is the mystery-of-mysteries, and that nothing measurable matters "a very good God damn": that "an artist, a man, a failure" is no mere whenfully accreting mechanism, but a givingly eternal complexity—neither some soulless and heartless ultrapredatory infra-animal nor any un-understandingly knowing and believing and thinking automaton, but a naturally and miraculously whole human being—a feelingly illimitable individual; whose only happiness is to transcend himself, whose every agony is to grow.

BIBLIOGRAPHICAL NOTE

FOR CONVENIENCE, I have placed all page references paren-
thetically in the text. If not specifically noted, the book referred
to should be clear from the context. Listed below are the volumes and editions consulted and used:

All of the poetry will be found in:

[a] *Poems 1923–1954*. New York: Harcourt, Brace, 1954.
[b] *95 Poems*. New York: Harcourt, Brace, 1958.

The prose works, listed chronologically, are as follows:

Anthropos: The Future of Art. Mount Vernon, N. Y.: Golden
    Eagle Press, 1944. Originally published 1930.
E. E. Cummings: A Miscellany, ed. George J. Firmage. New
    York: Argophile Press, 1958. Contains Cummings' essays
    dating back to 1915.
Eimi. New York: Grove Press Evergreen Paperback E-113,
    1958. Originally published 1933.
The Enormous Room. New York: Random House Modern Li-
    brary edition, 1934. Originally published 1922.
Him. New York: Liveright Publishing Co., 1927.
i:six nonlectures. Cambridge, Mass.: Harvard University Press,
    1953.
No Title. New York: Covici, Friede, 1930.
Santa Claus (A Morality), *Harvard Wake*, no. 5 (Cummings
    number, Spring 1946), 10–19. Published as a book by
    Henry Holt, 1946.
Tom. New York: Arrow Editions, 1935.

Posthumous works by Cummings:

Adventures in Value. Fifty Photographs by Marion Moore-
house. Text by E. E. Cummings. New York: Harcourt,
Brace & World, 1962.
Complete Poems 1913–1962. New York: Harcourt Brace Jo-
vanovich, 1972.
E. E. Cummings: A Miscellany Revised. George J. Firmage,
ed. New York: October House, 1965.
Fairy Tales. Illustrated by John Eaton. New York: Harcourt,
Brace & World, 1965.
Selected Letters of E. E. Cummings. F. W. Dupee and George
Stade, eds. New York: Harcourt, Brace & World, 1969.
73 Poems. New York: Harcourt, Brace & World, 1963.

Major publications about Cummings:

Baum, S. V., ed. *E&TI: e e c: E. E. Cummings and the Crit-
ics.* East Lansing: Michigan State University Press, 1962.
Dumas, Bethany K. *E. E. Cummings: A Remembrance of
Miracles.* New York: Barnes & Noble, 1974.
Eckley, Wilton. *The Merrill Checklist of E. E. Cummings.*
Columbus, Ohio: Charles E. Merrill, 1970.
_____. *The Merrill Guide to E. E. Cummings.* Columbus,
Ohio: Charles E. Merrill, 1970.
Fairley, Irene R. *E. E. Cummings and Ungrammar: A Study
of Syntactic Deviance in His Poems.* New York: Watermill,
1975.
Firmage, George J. *E. E. Cummings: A Bibliography.* Mid-
dletown, Conn.: Wesleyan University Press, 1960.
Friedman, Norman. *E. E. Cummings: The Art of His Poetry.*
Baltimore, Md.: Johns Hopkins University Press, 1960. Pa-
perback ed. 1967.
_____, ed. *E. E. Cummings: A Collection of Critical Essays.*
Englewood Cliffs, N. J.: Prentice-Hall, 1972.
Harvard Wake, no. 5 (Spring 1946). Special Cummings issue, guest editor José Villa.
Journal of Modern Literature, vol. 7, no. 2 (April 1979). Special Cummings issue, guest editor Richard S. Kennedy.

Kennedy, Richard S. *Dreams in the Mirror: A Biography of E. E. Cummings.* New York: Liveright, 1980.

Kidder, Rushworth M. *E. E. Cummings: An Introduction to the Poetry.* New York: Columbia University Press, 1979.

Lane, Gary. *I Am: A Study of E. E. Cummings' Poems.* Lawrence, Kan.: Regents Press of Kansas, 1976.

Marks, Barry A. *E. E. Cummings.* New York: Twayne, 1964.

Norman, Charles. *The Magic-Maker: E. E. Cummings.* New York: Macmillan, 1958. Rev. ed. New York: Duell, Sloane, & Pearce, 1964. Rev. and exp. ed. Indianapolis: Bobbs-Merrill, 1972.

Rotella, Guy L. *E. E. Cummings: A Reference Guide.* Boston: G. K. Hall, 1979.

Triem, Eve. *E. E. Cummings.* Minneapolis: University of Minnesota Press, 1969.

Wegner, Robert E. *The Poetry and Prose of E. E. Cummings.* New York: Harcourt, Brace & World, 1965.

INDEX

Page 137, line 11: *For* game, what *read* game,what

Page 155, lines 18–19 : *For* from my viewpoint,-makes *read* from my viewpoint,makes

Page 157, line 25: *For* dying is fine)but death *read* dying is fine)but Death

Page 189, column 1, lines 17–18: *For Anthropos: or The Future* of Art *read Anthropos: or The Future of Art*

Page 190, column 1, line 42: *For* "Dying is fine) but death," *read* "Dying is fine)but Death,"

Page 191, column 1, line 6: *For* "i am a little church (no *read* "i am a little church(no

Page 191, column 1, line 17: *For* "inthe, exquisite *read* "inthe,exquisite

Page 191, column 1, line 28: *For i: six nonlectures read i:six nonlectures*

Page 192, column 1, line 39: *For* Satie, Eric *read* Satie, Erik

Page 192, column 2, line 10: *For* "structure, miraculous" *read* "structure,miraculous"

Page 192, column 2, line 12: *For* "swi (/across!gold's," *read* "swi(/across!gold's,"

Page 13, line 12: *For* in term of *read* in terms of
Page 17, line 31: *For* a163) he *read* a163), he
Page 33, line 14: *For* nineteenth-century *read* eighteenth-centu
Page 39, line 27: *For* CHANSON INNOCENTES *read* CHANSONS INNOCENTS
Page 43, line 26: *For* appreciated, neither *read* appreciated: neit
Page 44, line 38: *For* to find it it's hollow *read* to find if it's hollo
Page 48, line 19: *For* TWO Contains *read* TWO contains
Page 48, line 22: *For* THREE Contains *read* THREE contains
Page 48, line 24: *For* FOUR Contains *read* FOUR contains
Page 48, line 25: *For* FIVE Contains *read* FIVE contains
Page 51, line 16: *For* (Norman, pp. 225–26) *read* (Norman, 19 pp. 225–26)
Page 51, lines 17–18: *For* let us resume *read* let us review
Page 53, line 9: *For* homageneous whole *read* homogeneous wh
Page 58, line 30: *For* HIM (standing *read* HIM (Standing
Page 60, line 1: *For* Mauer *read* Maurer
Page 73, line 14: *For* plays!) *read* play!)
Page 84, lines 25–26: *For* "Never to rest and never to have: only *read* "never to rest and never to have:only
Page 87, line 2: *For* because *read* that
Page 91, line 3: *For* Philistine who *read* Philistine, who
Page 116, lines 26–27: *For* not what anyone believes,-and *read* what anyone believes,and
Page 117, lines 3–4: *For* boxes are cages;-through *read* boxes are cages;through
Page 119, lines 11–12: *For* for he is doubt;-perfectly *read* for he i doubt;perfectly
Page 123, lines 33–34: *For* smell style:-touch something *read* sm style:touch something

Page 13, line 12: *For* in term of *read* in terms of
Page 17, line 31: *For* a163) he *read* a163), he
Page 33, line 14: *For* nineteenth-century *read* eighteenth-century
Page 39, line 27: *For* CHANSON INNOCENTES *read*
CHANSONS INNOCENTS
Page 43, line 26: *For* appreciated, neither *read* appreciated: neither
Page 44, line 38: *For* to find it it's hollow *read* to find if it's hollow
Page 48, line 19: *For* TWO Contains *read* TWO contains
Page 48, line 22: *For* THREE Contains *read* THREE contains
Page 48, line 24: *For* FOUR Contains *read* FOUR contains
Page 48, line 25: *For* FIVE Contains *read* FIVE contains
Page 51, line 16: *For* (Norman, pp. 225–26) *read* (Norman, 1958, pp. 225–26)
Page 51, lines 17–18: *For* let us resume *read* let us review
Page 53, line 9: *For* homageneous whole *read* homogeneous whole
Page 58, line 30: *For* HIM (standing *read* HIM (Standing
Page 60, line 1: *For* Mauer *read* Maurer
Page 73, line 14: *For* plays!) *read* play!)
Page 84, lines 25–26: *For* "Never to rest and never to have: only *read* "never to rest and never to have:only
Page 87, line 2: *For* because *read* that
Page 91, line 3: *For* Philistine who *read* Philistine, who
Page 116, lines 26–27: *For* not what anyone believes,-and *read* not what anyone believes,and
Page 117, lines 3–4: *For* boxes are cages;-through *read* boxes are cages;through
Page 119, lines 11–12: *For* for he is doubt;-perfectly *read* for he is doubt;perfectly
Page 123, lines 33–34: *For* smell style:-touch something *read* smell style:touch something

Page 137, line 11: *For* game, what *read* game,what

Page 155, lines 18–19 : *For* from my viewpoint,-makes *read* from my viewpoint,makes

Page 157, line 25: *For* dying is fine)but death *read* dying is fine)but Death

Page 189, column 1, lines 17–18: *For Anthropos: or The Future* of Art *read Anthropos: or The Future of Art*

Page 190, column 1, line 42: *For* "Dying is fine) but death," *read* "Dying is fine)but Death,"

Page 191, column 1, line 6: *For* "i am a little church (no *read* "i am a little church(no

Page 191, column 1, line 17: *For* "inthe, exquisite *read* "inthe,exquisite

Page 191, column 1, line 28: *For i: six nonlectures read i:six nonlectures*

Page 192, column 1, line 39: *For* Satie, Eric *read* Satie, Erik

Page 192, column 2, line 10: *For* "structure, miraculous" *read* "structure,miraculous"

Page 192, column 2, line 12: *For* "swi (/across!gold's," *read* "swi(/across!gold's,"